Hugo's Simplified System

Russian
Phrase Book

Hugo's Language Books Limited

This edition
© 1990 Hugo's Language Books Ltd/Lexus Ltd
All rights reserved
ISBN 0 85285 152 9

Compiled by
Lexus Ltd
with
Geoffrey and Ekaterina Smith

*Facts and figures given in this book were
correct when printed. If you discover any
changes, please write to us.*

3rd impression (with amendments) 1994

Set in 9/9 Plantin Light by
Typesetters Ltd and
printed by
Page Bros., Norwich

CONTENTS

Contents

PREFACE

This Russian Phrase Book has the same excellent pedigree as others in the Hugo series, having been compiled by experts to meet the general needs of tourists and business travellers. Inasmuch that your hotel room is likely to have been booked in advance, there's no need to say "Do you have two single rooms for one night?" – more probably you will want to say "The window's jammed" or "The light doesn't work".

Arranged under the usual headings of 'Hotels', 'Rail Travel' and so forth, the ample selection of useful words and phrases is supported by a 1960-line Mini-Dictionary which will help you form additional sentences (or at least express the one word you need!). There is also a section covering business vocabulary, and a Menu Guide listing some 300 dishes, drinks and basic foods.

Highlighted sections illustrate some of the replies you may be given, and the signs or instructions you may see or hear. All the principal word lists and phrases are printed in the Russian alphabet; like Greek, this can be fathomed without too much difficulty if you spend some time working on it before your trip. Moreover, you will be able to point to a phrase and get your message across. By using our system of imitated pronunciation, which follows each word or phrase, you should have no difficulty in reading the Russian, but if you use our audio cassette of selected extracts from the book, then you should be word-perfect! Ask your bookseller for the Hugo Russian Travel Pack.

The informative matter found in each chapter, and some items of vocabulary, have been fully revised in 1994 to reflect the recent changes that have taken place in Russia. For a while, however, there may be one or two spoken references to 'Leningrad' or 'the USSR' on the cassette, and for these we offer the listener – and all Russians – our apologies.

PRONUNCIATION

When reading the imitated pronunciation, stress that part which is underlined. Pronounce each syllable as if it formed part of an English word, and you will be understood sufficiently well. Remember the points below, and your pronunciation will be even closer to the correct Russian:

a	as in 'alimony'
ay	as in 'may'
e	as in 'egg'
I	as in 'die'
i	approximately as in 'lid'
kh	a guttural 'ch' as in the Scottish pronunciation of 'loch'
o	as in 'rob'
oy	as in 'boy'
s	as in 'lass'
ye	as in 'yet'
zh	as 's' in 'leisure' only harder
'	no sound of its own but softens the preceding consonant and adds a slight *y* sound, e.g. *n'* would sound *ny* as in 'canyon'.

The Mini-Dictionary provides the Russian translations in the form of the imitated pronunciation so that you can read the words without reference to the Russian alphabet. In the phrases, the abbreviations (*m*) and (*f*) indicate the forms to be used by a male or female speaker respectively.

On the next page is a further guide to Russian pronunciation, alongside the Russian (Cyrillic) alphabet. From this, you will see that there's no difficulty in reading signs in capital letters: apart from one (Б/б), they are all either mirror-versions of the small letters (Н/н) or like our own (А/а).

THE RUSSIAN (CYRILLIC) ALPHABET

letter		pronunciation
А	а	(a) as in 'alimony'
Б	б	(b) as in 'bed'
В	в	(v) as in 'vet'
Г	г	(g)/(v) as in 'get'/ 'vet'
Д	д	(d) as 'debt'
Е	е	(ye) as in 'yet'
Ё	ё	(yo) as in 'yonder'
Ж	ж	(zh) as in 'leisure', only rather harder
З	з	(z) as in 'zither'
И	и	(ee) as in 'see'
Й	й	(y) as in 'boy'
К	к	(k) as in 'king'
Л	л	(l) as in 'loot'
М	м	(m) as in 'match'
Н	н	(n) as in 'never'
О	о	(o) as in 'rob'
П	п	(p) as in 'pea'
Р	р	(r) as in 'rat-a-tat'
С	с	(s) as in 'lass'

letter		pronunciation
Т	т	(t) as in 'toffee'
У	у	(oo) as in 'boot'
Ф	ф	(f) as in 'fellow'
Х	х	(kh) as 'ch' in the Scottish 'loch'
Ц	ц	(ts) as in 'let's'
Ч	ч	(ch) as in 'chair'
Ш	ш	(sh) as in 'shovel'
Щ	щ	(shsh) as above but with a slight roll, as in 'fresh sheet'
Ъ	ъ	hard sign – no sound but use very slight pause before next letter
Ы	ы	(i) approximately as in 'lid'
Ь	ь	soft sign – no sound but softens preceding consonant
Э	э	(e) as in 'egg'
Ю	ю	(you) as in 'youth'
Я	я	(ya) as in 'yak'

USEFUL EVERYDAY PHRASES

Yes/no
Да/нет
da/nyet

Thank you
Спасибо
spaseeba

No thank you
Нет, спасибо
nyet, spaseeba

Please
Пожалуйста
pazhalsta

I don't understand
Я не понимаю
ya nye paneeta-yoo

Do you speak English?
Вы говорите по-английски?
vi gavareet-ye pa-angleeskee?

I can't speak Russian
Я не говорю по-русски
ya nye gavaryoo pa-rooskee

I don't know
Я не знаю
ya nye zna-yoo

Please speak more slowly
Пожалуйста, говорите медленнее
pazhalsta, gavareet-ye myedlyenye-ye

Please write it down for me
Пожалуйста, напишите это мне
pazhalsta, napeesheet-ye eta mnye

My name is...
Меня зовут...
myenya zavoot...

How do you do, pleased to meet you
Здравствуйте, очень приятно
zdrastvooyt-ye, ochyen' pree-yatna

Good morning
Доброе утро
dobra-ye ootra

Good afternoon
Добрый день
dobri dyen'

Good evening
Добрый вечер
dobri vyechyer

Good night (*when going to bed*)
Спокойной ночи
spakoynay nochee

Good night (*leaving group early*)
Счастливо оставаться!
shasleeva astavat'sa!

USEFUL EVERYDAY PHRASES

Goodbye
До свидания
da sveedanee-ya

How are you?
Как дела?
kak dyela?

Excuse me please
Извините, пожалуйста
eezveeneet-ye, pazhalsta

Sorry!
Простите!
prasteet-ye!

I'm really sorry
Я очень извиняюсь
ya ochyen' eezveenya-yoos'

Can you help me?
Вы можете мне помочь?
vi mozhet-ye mnye pamoch'?

Can you tell me...?
Скажите, пожалуйста...
skazheet-ye, pazhalsta...

Can I have...?
Можно...?
mozhna...?

I would like...
Я хотел (*m*)/хотела (*f*) бы...
ya khatyel/khatyela bi...

Is there... here?
Здесь есть...?
zdyes' yest'...?

Where can I get...?
Где можно найти...?
gdye mozhna nıtee...?

How much is it?
Сколько это стоит?
skol'ka eta sto-eet?

What time is it?
Который час?
katori chas?

I must go now
Мне пора идти
mnye para eetee

I've lost my way
Я заблудился (*m*)/заблудилась (*f*)
ya zabloodeelsa/zabloodeelas'

Cheers!
Ваше здоровье!
vashe zdarov'ye!

Do you take credit cards?
Вы принимаете кредитные карточки?
vi preeneema-yet-ye kryedeetniye kartachkee?

Where is the toilet?
Где туалет?
gdye too-alyet?

USEFUL EVERYDAY PHRASES

Go away!
Уходите!
ookhad<u>ee</u>t-ye!

Excellent!
Отлично!
atl<u>ee</u>chna!

THINGS YOU'LL HEAR

astar<u>o</u>zhna!	Look out!
ay!	Hey!
pazh<u>a</u>lsta	You're welcome
spas<u>ee</u>ba	Thanks
vot, pazh<u>a</u>lsta	Here you are
shto, prast<u>ee</u>t-ye?	Pardon?
kharash<u>o</u>, spas<u>ee</u>ba, a vi?	Fine, thank you – and you?
zdr<u>a</u>stvooyt-ye, <u>o</u>chyen' pr<u>ee</u>-yatna	How do you do, nice to meet you
oov<u>ee</u>deemsa p<u>o</u>zhe	See you later
kak dy<u>e</u>la?	How are you?
da sveed<u>a</u>nee-ya	Goodbye
prav<u>ee</u>l'na	That's right
pr<u>a</u>vda?	Is that so?
eezveen<u>ee</u>t-ye	Excuse me
ya nye pan<u>ee</u>ma-yoo	I don't understand
ya nye zn<u>a</u>-yoo	I don't know

THINGS YOU'LL SEE

вода для питья	*vada dlya peet'ya*	drinking water
вход	*fkhot*	way in/entrance
вход воспрещён	*fkhot vaspryeshyon*	no admittance
входите	*fkhadeet-ye*	come straight in
вход свободный	*fkhot svabodni*	admission free
выход	*vikhat*	way out/exit
Ж/женский туалет	*zhenskee too-alyet*	ladies
заказано	*zakazana*	reserved
закрыто	*zakrita*	closed
занято	*zanyata*	engaged
запасной выход	*zapasnoy vikhat*	emergency exit
Интурист	*eentooreest*	Intourist
касса	*kasa*	till
к себе	*ksyeb-ye*	pull
лифт	*leeft*	lift
М		underground; gentlemen
мужской туалет	*mooshskoy too-alyet*	gentlemen
осторожно, окрашено	*astarozhna, akrashena*	caution, wet paint
открыто	*atkrita*	open
от себя	*atsyebya*	push
пожарный выход	*pazharni vikhat*	fire exit
посторонним вход воспрещён	*pastaroneem fkhot vaspryeshyon*	private/no admittance
рынок	*rinak*	market
соблюдайте тишину	*sablyoodit-yet-ye teesheenoo*	silence/quiet
туалеты	*too-alyeti*	toilets
часы работы	*chasi raboti*	opening times

DAYS, MONTHS, SEASONS

Sunday	воскресенье	*vaskryesyen'ye*
Monday	понедельник	*panyedyel'neek*
Tuesday	вторник	*ftorneek*
Wednesday	среда	*sryeda*
Thursday	четверг	*chyetvyerk*
Friday	пятница	*pyatneetsa*
Saturday	суббота	*soobota*
January	январь	*yanvar'*
February	февраль	*fyevral'*
March	март	*mart*
April	апрель	*apryel'*
May	май	*mI*
June	июнь	*ee-yoon'*
July	июль	*ee-yool'*
August	август	*avgoost*
September	сентябрь	*syentyabr'*
October	октябрь	*aktyabr'*
November	ноябрь	*na-yabr'*
December	декабрь	*dyekabr'*
Spring	весна	*vyesna*
Summer	лето	*lyeta*
Autumn	осень	*osyen'*
Winter	зима	*zeema*
Christmas	Рождество	*razhdyestvo*
Christmas Eve	Сочельник	*sachyel'neek*
New Year	Новый год	*novi got*
New Year's Eve	Новогодняя ночь	*navagodnya-ya noch'*

NUMBERS

0 ноль *nol'*	**5** пять *pyat'*
1 один/одна/одно *adeen/adna/adno*	**6** шесть *shest'*
2 два/две *dva/dvye*	**7** семь *syem'*
3 три *tree*	**8** восемь *vosyem'*
4 четыре *chyetir-ye*	**9** девять *dyevyat'*

10 десять *dyesyat'*
11 одиннадцать *adeenatsat'*
12 двенадцать *dvyenatsat'*
13 тринадцать *treenatsat'*
14 четырнадцать *chyetirnatsat'*
15 пятнадцать *pyatnatsat'*
16 шестнадцать *shesnatsat'*
17 семнадцать *syemnatsat'*
18 восемнадцать *vasyemnatsat'*
19 девятнадцать *dyevyatnatsat'*
20 двадцать *dvatsat'*
21 двадцать один *dvatsat' adeen*
22 двадцать два *dvatsat' dva*
30 тридцать *treetsat'*
31 тридцать один *treetsat' adeen*
32 тридцать два *treetsat' dva*
40 сорок *sorak*
50 пятьдесят *pyadyesyat*
60 шестьдесят *shesdyesyat*
70 семьдесят *syem'dyesyat*
80 восемьдесят *vosyem'dyesyat*
90 девяносто *dyevyanosta*
100 сто *sto*
110 сто десять *sto dyesyat'*
200 двести *dvyestee*
300 триста *treesta*

NUMBERS

400 четыреста *chyetiryesta*
500 пятьсот *pyat'sot*
600 шестьсот *shes͞ot*
700 семьсот *syem'sot*
800 восемьсот *vasyem'sot*
900 девятьсот *dyevyat'sot*
1,000 тысяча *tisyacha*
10,000 десять тысяч *dyesyat' tisyach*
20,000 двадцать тысяч *dvatsat' tisyach*
100,000 сто тысяч *sto tisyach*
1,000,000 миллион *meelee-on*

ORDINAL NUMBERS

1st первое *pyerva-ye*
2nd второе *ftaro-ye*
3rd третье *tryet'ye*
4th четвёртое *chyetvyorta-ye*
5th пятое *pyata-ye*
6th шестое *shesto-ye*
7th седьмое *syed'mo-ye*
8th восьмое *vas'mo-ye*
9th девятое *dyevyata-ye*
10th десятое *dyesyata-ye*
11th одиннадцатое *adeenatsata-ye*
12th двенадцатое *dvyenatsata-ye*
13th тринадцатое *treenatsata-ye*
14th четырнадцатое *chyetirnatsata-ye*
15th пятнадцатое *pyatnatsata-ye*
16th шестнадцатое *shesnatsata-ye*
17th семнадцатое *syemnatsata-ye*
18th восемнадцатое *vasyemnatsata-ye*
19th девятнадцатое *dyevyatnatsata-ye*
20th двадцатое *dvatsata-ye*
21st двадцать первое *dvatsat' pyerva-ye*
30th тридцатое *treetsata-ye*
31st тридцать первое *treetsat' pyerva-ye*

TIME

today	сегодня	*syevodnya*
yesterday	вчера	*fchyera*
tomorrow	завтра	*zaftra*
the day before yesterday	позавчера	*pazafchyera*
the day after tomorrow	послезавтра	*paslyezaftra*
this week	на этой неделе	*na etay nyedyel-ye*
last week	на прошлой неделе	*na proshlay nyedyel-ye*
next week	на следующей неделе	*na slyedoo-yooshay nyedyel-ye*
this morning	сегодня утром	*syevodnya ootram*
this afternoon	сегодня днём	*syevodnya dnyom*
this evening/ tonight	сегодня вечером	*syevodnya vyechyeram*
yesterday afternoon	вчера днём	*fchyera dnyom*
last night (*before midnight*)	вчера вечером	*fchyera vyechyerom*
last night (*after midnight*)	вчера ночью	*fchyera noch'yoo*
tomorrow morning	завтра утром	*zaftra ootram*
tomorrow night	завтра вечером	*zaftra vyechyeram*
in three days	через три дня	*chyeryez tree dnya*
three days ago	три дня назад	*tree dnya nazat*
late	поздно	*pozna*
early	рано	*rana*
soon	скоро	*skora*
later on	позже	*pozhe*
at the moment	сейчас	*syaychas*
second	секунда	*syekoonda*
minute	минута	*meenoota*
one minute	одна минута	*adna meenoota*
two minutes	две минуты	*dvye meenooti*

quarter of an hour	четверть часа	*chyetvyert' chasa*
half an hour	полчаса	*palchasa*
three quarters of an hour	три четверти часа	*tree chyetvyertee chasa*
hour	час	*chas*
that day	этот день	*etat dyen'*
every day	каждый день	*kazhdi dyen'*
all day	весь день	*vyes' dyen'*
the next day	следующий день	*slyedoo-yooshee dyen'*

TELLING THE TIME

One o'clock is час (*chas*); for two, three and four o'clock use the number followed by часа (*chasa*); the remaining hours to twelve o'clock are simply the appropriate number plus the word часов (*chasov*).

For time past the hour, e.g. twenty past one, Russians say двадцать минут второго (*dvatsat' meenoot ftarova*) meaning literally "twenty minutes of the second (hour)". Quarter past and half past one are also expressed as being of the following hour. Quarter past one is therefore чертверть второго (*chyetvyert' ftarova*) and half past two is половина третьего (*palaveena tryet'yeva*).

For time to the hour Russians use без (*byez*) meaning "less", e.g. ten to three без десяти три (*byez dyesyatee tree*), literally "less ten three".

The 24-hour clock is commonly used, in particular for timetables. Cross-reference to the number section on page 15 may prove helpful.

am	утра	*ootra*
pm	дня	*dnya*
one o'clock	час	*chas*
ten past one	десять минут второго	*dyesyat' meenoot ftarova*
quarter past one	четверть второго	*chyetvyert' ftarova*

half past one	половина второго	*palaveena ftarova*
twenty to two	без двадцати два	*byez dvatsatee dva*
quarter to two	без четверти два	*byez chyetvyertee dva*
two o'clock	два часа	*dva chasa*
13.00	тринадцать ноль-ноль	*treenatsat' nol'-nol'*
16.30	шестнадцать тридцать	*shesnatsat' treetsat'*
at half past five	в половине шестого	*fpalaveen-ye shestova*
at seven o'clock	в семь часов	*fsyem' chasof*
noon	полдень	*poldyen'*
midnight	полночь	*polnach'*

HOTELS

In recent years the choice and standard of hotel accommodation in the big cities has improved significantly with the emergence of Western-managed hotels offering in general excellent standards of service. However, these are quite expensive and a typical package tour is more likely to involve a traditional Intourist hotel, particularly outside the big cities. This kind of package tour will usually include a generous, if not culinarily varied, breakfast, lunch and dinner plus a room with en-suite bathroom and telephone. Standards of service, courtesy and cleanliness vary but, compared to those of Western European hotels, are not likely to be more than adequate. Acting as a receptionist on each floor of the hotel, there will be a дежурная (*dyezhoorna-ya*) who will have custody of the keys and will issue a key-pass which will need to be shown when collecting the key. She will be able to help with any problem to do with your accommodation, laundry or simply make you a cup of tea.

Although it is now possible for foreigners to travel outside their principal area of residence (within the Russian Federation), without additional endorsement of their visa, advice should still be sought from your tour representative since some towns remain "closed" to foreign visitors.

Hotel guests are no exception to the general rule that travellers should always take a certain amount of foreign currency cash with them (preferably US dollars). You will need to exchange quite a lot of this foreign currency during your stay in Russia since shops, restaurants and bars will now only accept payment in roubles. Taxi drivers, however, may still expect you to pay in dollars.

Throughout the day it is usually possible to have a light snack and tea or coffee in one of the hotel cafeterias. Travellers requiring a vegetarian menu should notify the tour guide or inform the hotel staff when checking in.

USEFUL WORDS AND PHRASES

balcony	балкон	*balkon*
bathroom	ванная	*vana-ya*
bed	кровать	*kravat'*
bedroom	спальня	*spal'nya*
bill	счёт	*shyot*
breakfast	завтрак	*zaftrak*
dining room	столовая	*stalova-ya*
dinner	ужин	*oozheen*
double room	номер с двуспальной кроватью	*nomyer sdvoo-spal'nay kravat'yoo*
floor-lady	дежурная	*dyezhoorna-ya*
foyer	фойе	*ft-ye*
full board	проживание с трёхразовым питанием	*prazheevaneeye stryokh-razovim peetanee-yem*
half board	проживание с двухразовым питанием	*prazheevaneeye sdvookh-razovim peetanee-yem*
hotel	гостиница	*gasteeneetsa*
key	ключ	*klyooch*
lift	лифт	*leeft*
lunch	обед	*abyet*
manager	администратор	*admeeneestrator*
reception	регистратура	*ryegeestratoora*
restaurant	ресторан	*ryestaran*
room	номер	*nomyer*
room service	комнатное обслуживание	*komnatna-ye absloozheevaneeye*
shower	душ	*doosh*
single room	одноместный номер	*adnamyestni nomyer*
toilet	туалет	*too-alyet*
twin room	номер с двумя кроватями	*nomyer sdvoomya kravatyamee*

Do you have a larger/brighter room?
У вас есть номер побольше/посветлее?
oo vas yest' nomyer pabol'she/pasvyetlye-ye?

Please could I have the key for room number...?
Дайте, пожалуйста, ключ от номера...
dīt-ye, pazhalsta, klyooch ot nomyera...

There has been some mistake, I asked for a double room
Произошла ошибка, я просил (*m*)/просила (*f*) номер с
двуспальной кроватью
pra-eezashla asheepka, ya praseel/praseela nomyer sdvoo-spal'nay kravat'yoo

I'd prefer a room with a balcony
Я предпочёл (*m*)/предпочла (*f*) бы номер с балконом
ya pryedpachyol/pryedpachla bi nomyer sbalkonam

The window in my room is jammed
Окно в моём номере не открывается
akno vmayom nomyer-ye nye atkriva-yetsa

The shower doesn't work
Душ не работает
doosh nye rabota-yet

The bathroom light doesn't work
В ванной нет света
v-vanay nyet svyeta

Can I have another light bulb?
Дайте другую лампочку
dīt-ye droogoo-yoo lampachkoo

There is no hot water/toilet paper
Нет горячей воды/туалетной бумаги
nyet garyachyay vadi/ too-alyetnay boomagee

What is the charge per night?
Сколько стоит номер за ночь?
skol'ka sto-eet nomyer zanach'?

When is breakfast?
Когда завтрак?
kagda zaftrak?

Would you have my luggage brought up?
Будьте добры, принесите мой багаж
boo't-ye dabri, preenyeseet-ye moy bagazh

Please call me at... o'clock
Пожалуйста, позовите меня в... часов
pazhalsta, pazaveet-ye myenya v... chasof

Can I have breakfast in my room?
Можно завтракать в номере?
mozhna zaftrakat' vnomyer-ye?

I'll be back at... o'clock
Я вернусь в...
ya vyernoos' v...

My room number is...
Мой номер...
moy nomyer...

I'm leaving tomorrow.
Я уезжаю завтра
ya oo-yezha-yoo zaftra

At what time do I have to be out of my room?
Когда надо освободить номер?
kagda nada asvabadeet' nomyer?

Can I have the bill please?
Счёт, пожалуйста
shyot, pazhalsta

I'll pay by credit card
Я заплачу кредитной карточкой
ya zaplachoo kryedeetnay kartachkay

I'll pay cash
Я заплачу наличными
ya zaplachoo naleechnimee

Can you get me a taxi?
Вы можете вызвать мне такси?
vi mozhet-ye vizvat' mnye taksee?

Thank you for all your help
Спасибо за всю вашу помощь
spaseeba za fsyoo vashoo pomash'

THINGS YOU'LL HEAR

eezveeneet-ye, myest nyet
I'm sorry, we have no more places

adna-myestnikh namyerof bol'she nyet
There are no single rooms left

dvookh-myestnikh namyerof bol'she nyet
There are no double rooms left

na skol'ka nachyay?
For how many nights?

THINGS YOU'LL SEE

бар *bar*	bar
ванная *v<u>a</u>na-ya*	bath
гостиница *gast<u>ee</u>neetsa*	hotel
двухместный номер *dvookh-m<u>ye</u>stni* *n<u>o</u>myer*	double room
душ *doosh*	shower
завтрак *z<u>a</u>ftrak*	breakfast
заказ *zak<u>a</u>s*	reservation
запасной выход *zapasn<u>oy</u> vikhat*	emergency exit
к себе *ksyeb-ye*	pull
лифт *leeft*	lift
номер с двумя кроватями *n<u>o</u>myer* *sdvoom<u>ya</u> kr<u>a</u>vatyamee*	twin room
обед *ab<u>ye</u>t*	lunch
одноместный номер *adna-m<u>ye</u>stni* *n<u>o</u>myer*	single room
от себя *atsy<u>e</u>bya*	push
первый этаж *p<u>ye</u>rvi et<u>a</u>sh*	ground floor
пожарный выход *paz<u>h</u>arni vikhat*	fire exit
проживание с двухразовым питанием *prazheev<u>a</u>neeye sdvookh-r<u>a</u>zavim peet<u>a</u>nee-yem*	half board
проживание с трёхразовым питанием *prazheev<u>a</u>neeye stryokh-r<u>a</u>zavim peet<u>a</u>nee-yem*	full board
регистратура *ryegeestrat<u>oo</u>ra*	reception
ресторан *ryestar<u>a</u>n*	restaurant
счёт *shyot*	bill
туалет/W.C. *too-al<u>ye</u>t*	toilet
1	ground floor (*as shown on lift button*)

MOTORING

Apart from the usual documentation, i.e. an international driving licence (with enclosure in Russian) and insurance documentation, you will also need a car registration document and Intourist vehicle documentation. The latter will contain details of your itinerary and all stop-overs (as previously arranged). It will include vouchers for pre-paid accommodation and a car-sticker showing your country of origin.

Rough road conditions and relatively few garages make it essential to carry sufficient spares in case you have to do your own repairs, quite possibly in the back of beyond. Some important items worth taking are a spare plastic windscreen, tow rope, engine oil, brake fluid, jump start leads, spark plugs, spare windscreen wipers, spare bulbs, electric points and fuses, antifreeze in winter and a luminous warning triangle to place on the road in case you break down. Because it cannot be taken for granted that all garages sell the right petrol for your car, it is also worth taking a couple of cans of petrol to stock up when you can and thus always have emergency supplies with you.

On the open road international (diagrammatic) road signs are used. The traffic police are called ГАИ (*Ga-ee*), which stands for State Automobile Inspectorate. If lost or in need of help they can, sometimes, be helpful. Drive on the right and overtake on the left. On main roads out of town the speed limit is generally 110 kph, and in town it is generally 60 kph. Front passengers must wear their seat belts. It is a crime to drive a car after drinking any alcohol.

SOME COMMON ROAD SIGNS

автостанция	*afta-stantsee-ya*	garage
автостоянка	*afta-sta-yanka*	car park

автострада *afta-strada*	motorway
бензоколонка *byenzakalonka*	petrol station
берегись поезда *byeryegees' po-yezda*	beware of trains
включить фары *vklyoocheet' fari*	headlights on
внимание! *vneemaneeye!*	watch out!
вход воспрещён *vkhod vuspryeshyon*	no tresspassing
выключить фары *viklyoocheet' fari*	headlights off
въезд запрещён *v-yest zapryeshyon*	no entry
гололёд *galalyot*	sheet ice
держитесь левой стороны *dyerzheetyes' lyevay starani*	(*pedestrians*) keep to the left
дорожные работы *darozhniye raboti*	roadworks
ж/д переезд *zhe de pyerye-yest*	level crossing
железнодорожный переезд *zhelyezna-darozhni pyerye-yest*	level crossing
зона *zona*	zone
конец автострады *kanyets afta-stradi*	end of motorway
медленно *myedlyena*	slow
не обгонять *nye abganyat'*	no overtaking
объезд *ab-yest*	diversion
одностороннее движение *adna-staronye-ye dveezheneeye*	one-way street
опасно *apasna*	danger
опасный перекрёсток *apasni pyeryekryostak*	dangerous junction
опасный поворот *apasni pavarot*	dangerous bend
осторожно *astarozhna*	caution
перекрёсток *pyeryekryostak*	crossroads
пешеходы *pyeshekhodi*	pedestrians
подземный переход *padzyemni pyeryekhot*	subway
скользко *skol'zka*	slippery surface
скорая помощь *skora-ya pomash'*	first-aid
станция техобслуживания *stantsee-ya tyekh-absloozheevanee-ya*	service station

→

27

стоянка запрещена *sta-yanka zapryeshena*		no parking
центр города *tsyentr gorada*		town centre
школа *shkola*		school

USEFUL WORDS AND PHRASES

antifreeze	антифриз	*anteefrees*
automatic	автоматический	*afta-mateechyeskee*
boot	багажник	*bagazhneek*
breakdown	поломка	*palomka*
brake (*noun*)	тормоз	*tormas*
car	машина	*masheena*
caravan	дом-автофургон	*dom-aftafoorgon*
clutch	сцепление	*stsyeplyeneeye*
crossroads	перекрёсток	*pyeryekryostak*
to drive	водить машину	*vadeet' masheenoo*
engine	мотор	*mator*
exhaust	выхлопная труба	*vikhlapna-ya trooba*
fanbelt	вентиляционный ремень	*vyenteelyatsee-oni ryemyen'*
garage (*for repairs*)	автостанция	*afta-stantsee-ya*
garage (*for petrol*)	бензоколонка	*byenzakalonka*
gear	передача	*pyeryedacha*
headlights	фары	*fari*
junction (*on motorway*)	развилка	*razveelka*
licence	водительские права	*vadeetyel'skeeye prava*
rear lights	задние фонари	*zadneeye fanaree*
lorry	грузовик	*groozaveek*
motoring manual	автомобильный справочник	*aftamabeel'ni spravachneek*
mirror	зеркало	*zyerkala*

28

motorbike	мотоцикл	*matatseekl*
motorway	автострада	*afta-strada*
number plate	номерной знак	*namyernoy znak*
petrol	бензин	*byenzeen*
road	дорога	*daroga*
to skid	заносить	*zanaseet'*
spares	запчасти	*zapchastee*
speed (*noun*)	скорость	*skorast'*
speed limit	ограничение	*agraneechyeneeye*
	скорости	*skorastee*
speedometer	спидометр	*speedomyetr*
steering wheel	руль	*rool'*
to tow	буксировать	*bookseeravat'*
traffic lights	светофор	*sfyetafor*
trailer	прицеп	*preetsyep*
tyre	шина	*sheena*
van	фургон	*foorgon*
wheel	колесо	*kalyeso*
windscreen	переднее стекло	*pyeryednye-ye*
		styeklo

I'd like some oil/water
Мне нужно масло/нужна вода
mnye noozhna masla/noozhna vada

Fill her up please!
Полный бак, пожалуйста!
polni bak, pazhalsta!

I'd like 10 litres of petrol
Мне нужно 10 литров бензина
mnye noozhna dyesyat' leetraf byenzeena

Would you check the tyres please?
Проверьте шины, пожалуйста
pravyer't-ye sheeni, pazhalsta

MOTORING

Do you do repairs?
Здесь можно починить машину?
zdyes' mozhna pacheeneet' masheenoo?

Can you repair the brakes?
Вы можете починить тормоза?
vi mozhet-ye pacheeneet' tarmaza?

How long will it take?
Сколько времени это займёт?
skol'ka vryemyenee eta zimyot?

Where can I park?
Где можно поставить машину?
gdye mozhna pastaveet' masheenoo?

Can I park here?
Можно здесь поставить машину?
mozhna zdyes' pastaveet' masheenoo?

There is something wrong with the engine
Что-то случилось с мотором
shto-ta sloocheelas' smatoram

The engine is overheating
Мотор перегревается
mator pyerye-gryeva-yetsa

I need a new tyre
Мне нужна новая шина
mnye noozhna nova-ya sheena

I'd like to hire a car
Я хочу взять напрокат машину
ya khachoo vzyat' naprakat masheenoo

Where is the nearest garage?
Где ближайшая автостанция?
gdye bleezhisha-ya afta-stantsee-ya?

How do I get to...?
Как доехать до...?
kak da-yekhat' do...?

Is this the road to...?
Это дорога в...?
eta daroga v...?

DIRECTIONS YOU MAY BE GIVEN

pryama	straight on
slyeva	on the left
pavyerneet-ye nalyeva	turn left
sprava	on the right
pavyerneet-ye naprava	turn right
pyervi pavarot naprava	first on the right
ftaroy pavarot nalyeva	second on the left
posl-ye...	past the...

THINGS YOU'LL HEAR

vi khateet-ye afta-mateechyeskee eelee roochnoy?
Would you like an automatic or a manual?

pakazheet-ye vashee prava
May I see your licence?

THINGS YOU'LL SEE

бензин	*byenzeen*	petrol
выход	*vikhat*	exit
давление в шинах	*davlyeneeye fsheenakh*	tyre pressure
дизель	*deezyel'*	diesel
масло	*masla*	oil
развилка	*razveelka*	motorway junction
ремонт	*ryemont*	repair

RAIL TRAVEL

Train travel in Russia will give even the most sanitized tour package a true flavour of the apalling grime of day-to-day conditions and the magnificent warmth of the people who have to live in them. Apart from transporting you from A to D, train journeys should also be seized as an excellent opportunity for getting to know the Russians and speak Russian with them.

On long distance journeys, tourists will travel in мягкий (*myakhkee*; literally "soft") compartments with two sleeping berths in first class and four in second class. All compartments are non-smokers unless passengers agree to the contrary.

The carriage attendant is there as a sort of maître d'hôtel cum chambermaid. He or she is responsible for (and house-proud of) the cleanliness of the carriage, and also makes up the beds, sorts out the rowdies, and serves tea. When not busy working (and frequently also when they are), they usually enjoy a good chat.

To avoid wasting time on buying tickets for long-distance journeys, it is always worth booking a seat through Intourist. Buying tickets for suburban trains, on the other hand, can be done as easily as in the West.

USEFUL WORDS AND PHRASES

booking office	касса	*kasa*
buffet	буфет	*boofyet*
carriage	вагон	*vagon*
compartment	купе	*koope*
connection	пересадка	*pyeryesatka*
dining car	вагон-ресторан	*vagon-ryestaran*
emergency cord	стоп-кран	*stop-kran*
entrance	вход	*fkhot*
exit	выход	*vikhot*
first class	первый класс	*pyervi klas*

to get in	входить	*fkhadeet'*
to get out	выходить	*vikhadeet'*
guard	проводник	*pravadneek*
indicator board	табло	*tablo*
left luggage office	камера хранения	*kamyera khranyenee-ya*
lost property office	бюро находок	*byooro nakhodak*
luggage rack	багажная полка	*bagazhna-ya polka*
luggage trolley	тележка для багажа	*tyelyeshka dlya bagazha*
luggage van	багажное отделение	*bagazhna-ye atdyelyeneeye*
platform	платформа	*platforma*
by rail	поездом	*po-yezdam*
railway	железная дорога	*zhelyezna-ya daroga*
reserved seat	забронированное место	*zabraneeravana-ye myesta*
restaurant car	вагон-ресторон	*vagon-ryestaran*
return ticket	обратный билет	*abratni beelyet*
seat	место	*myesta*
second class	второй класс	*ftaroy klas*
single ticket	билет в один конец	*beelyet vadeen kanyets*
sleeping car	спальный вагон	*spal'ni vagon*
station (*main-line terminal*)	вокзал	*vagzal*
station (*all other stations*)	станция	*stantsee-ya*
station master	начальник вокзала	*nachal'neek vagzala*
ticket	билет	*beelyet*
ticket collector	контролёр	*kantralyor*
timetable	расписание	*raspeesaneeye*
tracks	пути	*pootee*
train	поезд	*po-yest*
waiting room	зал ожидания	*zal azheedanee-ya*
window	окно	*akno*

When does the train for... leave?
Когда отходит поезд в...?
kagda atkhodeet po-yest v...?

When does the train from... arrive?
Когда приходит поезд из...?
kagda preekhodeet po-yest eez...?

When is the next train to...?
Когда следующий поезд в...?
kagda slyedoo-yooshee po-yest v...?

When is the first train to...?
Когда первый поезд в...?
kagda pyervi po-yest v...?

When is the last train to...?
Когда последний поезд в...?
kagda paslyednee po-yest v...?

What is the fare to...?
Сколько стоит проезд до...?
skol'ka sto-eet pro-yest do...?

Do I have to change?
Мне нужно делать пересадку?
mnye noozhna dyelat' pyeryesatkoo?

Does the train stop at...?
Поезд останавливается в...?
po-yest astanavleeva-yetsa v...?

How long does it take to get to...?
Сколько времени нужно ехать до...?
skol'ka vryemyenee noozhna yekhat' do...?

RAIL TRAVEL

A return ticket to..., please
Обратный билет до..., пожалуйста
abratni beelyet do..., pazhalsta

Do I have to pay a supplement?
Я должен (*m*)/должна (*f*) доплатить?
ya dolzhen/dalzhna daplateet'?

I'd like to reserve a seat
Я хочу заказать место
ya khachoo zakazat' myesta

Is this the right train for...?
Это поезд до...?
eta po-yest do...?

Is this the right platform for the... train?
С этой платформы отходит поезд до...?
setay platformi atkhodeet po-yest do...?

Which platform for the... train?
С какой платформы отходит поезд до...?
skakoy platformi atkhodeet po-yest do...?

Is the train late?
Поезд опаздывает?
po-yest apazdiva-yet?

Could you help me with my luggage, please?
Вы не поможете мне с багажом, пожалуйста
vi nye pamozhet-ye mnye sbagazhom, pazhalsta

Is this seat free?
Это место свободно?
eta myesta svabodna?

This seat is taken
Это место занято
eta myesta zanyata

I have reserved this seat
Я забронировал (*m*)/забронировала (*f*) это место
ya zabraneeraval/zabraneeravala eta myesta

May I open the window?
Можно открыть окно?
mozhna atkrit' akno?

May I close the window?
Можно закрыть окно?
mozhna zakrit' akno?

When do we arrive in...?
Когда мы приезжаем в...?
kagda mi pree-yezha-yem v...?

What station is this?
Какая это станция?
kaka-ya eta stantsee-ya?

What station is this?
Какой это вокзал?
kakoy eta vagzal?

Do we stop at...?
Мы останавливаемся в...?
mi astanavleeva-yemsa v...?

Would you keep an eye on my things for a moment?
Вы не посмотрите минуту за моими вещами?
vi nye pasmotreet-ye meenootoo za ma-eemee vyeshamee?

37

Is there a restaurant car on this train?
В этом поезде есть вагон-ресторан?
vetam po-yezd-ye yest' vagon-ryestaran?

THINGS YOU'LL SEE

билетная касса *beelyetna-ya kasa*	ticket office
билеты *beelyeti*	tickets
буфет *boofyet*	snack bar
вагон *vagon*	carriage
вокзал *vagzal*	central station
воскресенья и выходные дни *vaskryesyen'ya ee vikhadniye dnee*	Sundays and public holidays
вход *fkhot*	entrance
выход *vikhat*	exit
газеты *gazyeti*	newspapers
доплата *daplata*	supplement
задержка *zadyershka*	delay
зал ожидания *zal azheedanee-ya*	waiting room
занято *zanyata*	engaged
информация *eenformatsee-ya*	information
камера хранения *kamyera khranyenee-ya*	left luggage
к поездам *k po-yezdam*	to the trains
кроме воскресений *krom-ye vaskryesyenee*	Sundays excepted
место для курения *myesta dlya kooryenee-ya*	smoking permitted
не высовываться из окон *nye visovivat'sa eez okan*	do not lean out of the window

38

не курить *nye kooreet'*	no smoking
не останавливается в... *nye astanavleeva-yetsa v...*	does not stop in...
нет входа *nyet fkhoda*	no entry
обмен валюты *abmyen valyooti*	currency exchange
отправление *atpravlyeneeye*	departures
платформа *platforma*	platform
поездка *pa-yestka*	journey
предварительный заказ билетов *pryedvareetyel'ni zakas beelyetaf*	seat reservation
прибытие *preebiteeye*	arrivals
пригородный поезд *preegaradni po-yest*	local train
расписание *raspeesaneeye*	timetable
свободно *svabodna*	vacant
спальный вагон *spal'ni vagon*	sleeping car
стоп-кран *stop-kran*	emergency cord
только по будним дням *tol'ka paboodneem dnyam*	weekdays only

THINGS YOU'LL HEAR

vneemaneeye
Attention

beelyeti, pazhalsta
Tickets please

AIR TRAVEL

All internal flights in Russia are made either with the state airline, Aeroflot or a new private airline called Transaero. Bookings are usually made through Intourist. Check that you have all necessary flight information, and in any case of doubt ask Intourist to provide you with flight details in English and, if possible, in writing.

Before making arrangements to fly in Russia, you should first check that your visa permits you to travel to where you want to go. If it doesn't, ask Intourist what to do to get authorisation. Be sure that you receive your ticket in good time and fully understand the flight details. You should make all necessary arrangements for accommodation prior to departure.

USEFUL WORDS AND PHRASES

aircraft	самолёт	*samalyot*
airline	воздушная линия	*vazdooshna-ya leenee-ya*
airport	аэропорт	*aeraport*
arrival	прибытие	*preebiteeye*
baggage claim	выдача багажа	*vidacha bagazha*
boarding card	посадочный талон	*pasadachni talon*
check-in (*noun*)	регистрация	*ryegeestratsee-ya*
check-in desk	стойка регистрации	*stoyka ryegeestratsee-ee*
customs	таможня	*tamozhnya*
delay	задержка	*zadyershka*
departure	отправление	*atpravlyeneeye*
departure lounge	зал вылета	*zal vilyeta*
emergency exit	запасной выход	*zapasnoy vikhat*
fire exit	пожарный выход	*pazharni vikhat*
flight	рейс	*ryays*
flight number	рейс номер	*ryays nomyer*

gate	выход на посадку	*vikhat na pasatkoo*
jet	реактивный самолёт	*rye-akteevni samalyot*
land (*verb*)	приземлиться	*preezyemleet'sa*
long distance flight	рейс дальнего следования	*ryays dal'nyeva slyedavanee-ya*
passport	паспорт	*paspart*
passport control	паспортный контроль	*paspartni kantrol'*
pilot	пилот	*peelot*
runway	взлётно-посадочная полоса	*vzlyotna-pasadachna-ya palasa*
seat	место	*myesta*
seat belt	ремень	*ryemyen'*
steward	борт-проводник	*bart-pravadneek*
stewardess	стюардесса	*styoo-ardyesa*
take-off (*noun*)	взлёт	*vzlyot*
window	окно	*akno*
wing	крыло	*krilo*

When is there a flight to...?
Когда рейс в...?
kagda ryays v...?

What time does the flight to... leave?
Когда вылетает самолёт в...?
kagda vilyeta-yet samalyot v...?

Is it a direct flight?
Это прямой рейс?
eta pryamoy ryays?

Do I have to change planes?
Я должен (*m*)/должна (*f*) пересесть на другой самолёт?
ya dolzhen/dalzhna pyeryesyest' na droogoy samalyot?

When do I have to check in?
Когда я должен (*m*)/должна (*f*) быть в аэропорту для регистрации?
kagda ya dolzhen/dalzhna bit' vaeraportoo dlya ryegeestratsee-ee?

I'd like a single ticket to...
Дайте, пожалуйста, один билет до...
dIt-ye, pazhalsta, adeen beelyet do...

I'd like a return ticket to...
Дайте, пожалуйста, обратный билет до...
dIt-ye, pazhalsta, abratni beelyet do...

I'd like a non-smoking seat
Я хочу место в отделении для некурящих
ya khachoo myesta vatdyelyenee-ee dlya nyekooryasheekh

I'd like a window seat please
Я хочу место у окна, пожалуйста
ya khachoo myesta oo akna, pazhalsta

How long will the flight be delayed?
На сколько задерживается рейс?
na skol'ka zadyerzheeva-yetsa ryays?

Which gate for the flight to...?
Какой выход на посадку на рейс до...?
kakoy vikhat na pasatkoo na ryays do...?

When do we arrive in...?
Когда мы прибываем в...?
kagda mi preebiva-yem v...?

May I smoke now?
Теперь можно курить?
tyepyer' mozhna kooreet'?

I do not feel very well
Мне плохо
mnye plokha

THINGS YOU'LL SEE

Аэрофлот *aeraflot*	Aeroflot
борт-проводник *bart-pravadneek*	steward
выдача багажа *vidacha bagazha*	baggage claim
вынужденная посадка *vinoozhdyena-ya pasatka*	emergency landing
высота *visata*	altitude
выход на посадку *vikhat na pasatkoo*	gate
задержка *zadyershka*	delay
запасной выход *zapasnoy vikhat*	emergency exit
информация *eenfarmatsee-ya*	information
местное время *myestna-ye vryemya*	local time
не курить *nye kooreet'*	no smoking
отправление *atpravlyeneeye*	departures
паспортный контроль *paspartni kantrol'*	passport control
пассажиры *pasazheeri*	passengers
пожарный выход *pazharni vikhat*	fire exit
прибытие *preebiteeye*	arrivals
пристегните ремни *pree-styegneet-ye ryemnee*	fasten seat belts
прямой рейс *pryamoy ryays*	direct flight
регистрация *ryegeestratsee-ya*	check-in
регулярный рейс *ryegoolyarni ryays*	scheduled flight
рейс *ryays*	flight
самолёт *samalyot*	aircraft
скорость *skorast'*	speed
стюардесса *styoo-ardyesa*	stewardess

→

43

таможенный контроль	*tamozheni kantrol'*	customs control
транзитная посадка	*tranzeetna-ya pasatka*	intermediate stop
явиться на регистрацию	*yaveet'sa na ryegeestratsee-yoo*	to check in

---

THINGS YOU'LL HEAR

abyavlya-yetsa pasatka na ryays...
The flight for... is now boarding

pazhalsta, prideet-ye na pasatkoo k vikhadoo nomyer...
Please go now to gate number...

LOCAL PUBLIC TRANSPORT AND TAXIS

A single ride on a bus, tram or trolleybus costs a flat fare equivalent to no more than a few pence. Single tickets are no longer sold on the vehicle, so get your tickets in a booklet of ten, called a книжечка (*kneezhechka*), which can be bought from the driver or a newspaper kiosk. Validate your ticket for the ride by perforating it in one of the punches hanging from the wall.

Bus stops have a yellow sign marked "A" and trolleybus stops have a white sign marked "T". These transport services and the underground run from about 6am to about 12pm. For people staying in Moscow or St. Petersburg for three or more weeks, it may be worth getting a monthly season ticket – единый (*yedeeni*) – which is valid on all forms of public transport, including the underground. The *yedeeni,* however, is only valid for a calendar month (so from mid-January to mid-February it probably would not be worth having because you would need to buy two).

Plastic underground tokens – жетоны (*zhetoni*) – costing the equivalent of a few pence are bought from ticket offices in the station. Feed a token into the slot by the red light at the automatic barrier and you are then entitled to travel wherever you want until your ride is ended. To leave the underground follow the выход в город (*vikhat vgorat*) signs, which mean "Exit to the city".

Whenever using the underground it is probably worth writing down the name of your destination to help identify it in Cyrillic. To change lines, look for the sign переход на поезда до станций... (*pyeryekhod na pa-yezda do stantsee...*), meaning "Change to trains for stations.."

Available taxis can be identified by a green light in the front of the windscreen. Frequently, unofficial taxi-drivers offer to pick you up, but in all such cases it is wise to fix the price in advance (or if you are clearly being fleeced at the other end, proffer no more than a reasonable maximum, forget all your

Russian and depart expressing bewilderment and indignation in English). Treat tipping just as you would do at home.

Some of the expressions below would be suitable for travellers going on a boat-trip.

USEFUL WORDS AND PHRASES

adult	взрослый	*vzrosli*
bus	автобус	*aftoboos*
bus stop	остановка автобуса	*astanofka aftoboosa*
child	ребёнок	*ryebyonak*
coach	автобус	*aftoboos*
conductor	кондуктор	*kandooktar*
connection	пересадка	*pyeryesatka*
cruise	круиз	*kroo-eez*
driver	водитель	*vadeetyel'*
fare	стоимость проезда	*sto-eemast' pra-yezda*
ferry	паром	*parom*
lake	озеро	*ozyera*
network map	схема	*skhyema*
number 5 bus	пятый автобус	*pyati aftoboos*
passenger	пассажир	*pasazheer*
quay	пристань	*preestan'*
river	река	*ryeka*
sea	море	*mor-ye*
seat	место	*myesta*
ship	теплоход	*tyeplakhot*
station	станция	*stantsee-ya*
subway	подземный переход	*padzyemni pyeryekhot*
taxi	такси	*taksee*
terminus	конечный пункт	*kanyechni poonkt*
ticket	билет	*beelyet*
tram	трамвай	*tramvi*
underground	метро	*myetro*

Where is the nearest underground station?
Где ближайшая станция метро?
gdye bleezhīsha-ya stantsee-ya myetro?

Where is the bus station?
Где автобусная станция?
gdye aftoboosna-ya stantsee-ya?

Where is there a bus stop?
Где остановка автобуса?
gdye astanofka aftoboosa?

Which buses go to...?
Какие автобусы идут до...?
kakeeye aftoboosi eedoot do...?

How often do the buses go to...?
Как часто ходят автобусы в...?
kak chasta khodyat aftoboosi v...?

Would you tell me when we get to...?
Скажите, пожалуйста, когда мы приедем в...?
skazheet-ye, pazhalsta, kagda mi pree-yedyem v...?

Do I have to get off yet?
Мне пора выходить?
mnye para vikhadeet'?

How do you get to...?
Как добраться до...?
kak dabrat'sa do...?

Is it very far?
Это далеко ?
eta dalyeko?

I want to go to...
Я хочу поехать в...
ya khachoo pa-yekhat' v...

Do you go near...?
Вы едете в сторону...?
vi yedyet-ye fstoranoo...?

Where can I buy a ticket?
Где можно купить билет?
gdye mozhna koopeet' beelyet?

Could you close/open the window?
Закройте/откройте окно, пожалуйста
zakroyt-ye/atkroyt-ye akno, pazhalsta

Could you help me get a ticket?
Вы не поможете мне купить билет?
vi nye pamozhet-ye mnye koopeet' beelyet?

When does the last bus leave?
Когда отходит последний автобус?
kagda atkhodeet paslyednee aftoboos?

THINGS YOU'LL HEAR

beelyeti, pazhalsta
Tickets, please

astarozhna, dvyeree zakriva-yootsa!
Be careful, the doors are closing!

slyedoo-yoosha-ya stantsee-ya...
The next station is...

THINGS YOU'LL SEE

билет *beelyet*	ticket
взрослые *vzrosliye*	adults
вход *fkhot*	entrance
дети *dyetee*	children
запасной выход *zapasnoy vikhat*	emergency exit
конечный пункт *kanyechni poonkt*	terminus
контролёр *kantralyor*	ticket inspector
маршрут *marshroot*	route
места *myesta*	seats
мест нет *myest nyet*	full
не курить *nye kooreet'*	no smoking
нет входа *nyet fkhoda*	no entry
остановка *astanofka*	stop
отправление *atpravlyeneeye*	departures
пожарный выход *pazharni vikhat*	fire exit
разговаривать с водителем запрещается *razgavareevat' svadeetyelyem zapryesha-yetsa*	do not speak to the driver
стоянка такси *sta-yanka taksee*	taxi rank

DOING BUSINESS

In addition to the usual information, your business card should state how you can be contacted from Russia. It is a good idea to have your business card and any literature about your company in both English and Russian. Owing to the chronic shortage of public telephone lines and the slowness of the postal service, you should consider establishing an alternative means of communication such as fax, telex or a private line.

If your delegation does not have a Russian speaker, make sure in advance that the Russian side will supply sufficient qualified translators at all meetings.

It will be handy to have some gifts with you for appropriate occasions, especially gifts with obvious Western kudos such as high-tech gadgets or Scotch whisky. Even more than in the West, the key figure to impress is the top man. He and his senior colleagues should be treated with particular attentiveness, wherever possible by representatives of corresponding rank from your own company.

Clearly, personal tact and business experience best dictate how to handle personal relationships with your Russian partners. Do not insult them by arguing over payment for any hospitality they are providing. Equally, do not take for granted how attractive they find contacts with Westerners. Apart from a widespread partiality for Western consumer goods, mention of future business trips to the West is, where appropriate, likely to prove a strong incentive to them to continue business relations.

USEFUL WORDS AND PHRASES

accept	принимать	*preeneemat'*
accountant	бухгалтер	*bookhgaltyer*
accounts department	бухгалтерия	*bookhgaltyeree-ya*
to advertise	рекламировать	*ryeklameeravat'*

advertisement	реклама	*ryeklama*
airfreight	воздушная доставка	*vazdooshna-ya dastafka*
bid	заявка	*za-yafka*
board (of directors)	правление (директоров)	*pravlyeneeye (deeryektarof)*
brochure	брошюра	*brashyoora*
business card	карточка (бизнесмена)	*kartachka (beeznyesmyena)*
chairman	председатель	*pryedsyedatyel'*
cheap	дешёвый	*dyeshyovi*
client	клиент	*klee-yent*
company	компания	*kampanee-ya*
computer	компьютер	*kampyootyer*
consumer	потребитель	*patryebeetyel'*
contract	договор	*dagavor*
cost	стоимость	*sto-eemast'*
customer	покупатель	*pakoopatyel'*
director	директор	*deeryektar*
discount	скидка	*skeetka*
documents	документы	*dakoomyenti*
down payment	аванс	*avans*
engineer	инженер	*eenzhenyer*
executive	исполнитель	*eespalneetyel'*
expensive	дорогой	*daragoy*
exports	экспорты	*eksporti*
fax	факсимильный аппарат	*fakseemeelni aparat*
to import	импортировать	*eemporteeravat'*
imports	импорты	*eemporti*
instalment	очередной взнос	*achyeryednoy vznos*
invoice	накладная	*nakladna-ya*
to invoice	послать накладную	*paslat' nakladnoo-yoo*
letter	письмо	*pees'mo*
letter of credit	кредитное письмо	*kryedeetna-ye pees'mo*

loss	ущерб	*oosherp*
manager	управляющий	*oopravlya-yooshee*
manufacture	изготовление	*eezgatavlyeneeye*
margin	запас	*zapas*
market	рынок	*rinak*
marketing	продажа	*pradazha*
meeting	собрание	*sabraneeye*
negotiations	переговоры	*pyeryegavori*
offer	предложение	*pryedlazheneeye*
order	заказ	*zakas*
to order	заказывать	*zakazivat'*
personnel	персонал	*pyersanal*
price	цена	*tsena*
product	продукция	*pradooktsee-ya*
production	производство	*pra-eezvotstva*
profit	прибыль	*preebil'*
promotion	продвижение	*pradveezheneeye*
(*publicity*)	с помощью	*spomash'yoo*
	рекламы	*ryeklami*
purchase order	закупочный заказ	*zakoopachni zakas*
sales department	отдел продажи	*atdyel pradazhee*
sales director	директор по	*deeryektar po*
	продаже	*pradazhe*
sales figures	статистика	*stateesteeka*
	продажи	*pradazhee*
secretary	секретарь (*m*)/	*syekryetar'/*
	секретарша (*f*)	*syekryetarsha*
shipment	доставка морем	*dastafka moryem*
tax	налог	*nalok*
telex	телекс	*tyelyeks*
tender (*noun*)	посыльное судно	*pasil'na-ye soodna*
total	итог	*eetok*

My name is...
Меня зовут...
myenya zavoot...

Here's my card
Вот моя карточка
vot ma-ya kartachka

Pleased to meet you
Рад (*m*)/рада (*f*) познакомиться
rad/rada paznakomeet'sa

May I introduce...?
Позвольте представить...
pazvol't-ye pryedstaveet'...

My company is...
Моя компания...
ma-ya kampanee-ya...

Our product is selling very well in the UK market
Наша продукция очень хорошо продаётся на британском
рынке
*nasha pradooktsee-ya ochyen' kharasho prada-yotsa na
breetanskam rink-ye*

We are looking for partners in Russia
Мы ищем партнёров в России
mi eeshem partnyoraf vrasee

At our last meeting...
На нашей последней встрече...
na nashay paslyednay fstryeche...

10/25/50 per cent
десять/двадцать пять/пятьдесят процентов
dyesyat'/dvatsat' pyat'/pyadyesyat pratsentaf

More than...
Больше чем...
bol'she chyem...

Less than...
Меньше чем...
myenshe chyem...

We're on schedule
Мы выполняем сроки
mi vipalnya-yem srokee

We're slightly behind schedule
Мы немного отстаём от сроков
mi nyemnoga atsta-yom atsrokaf

Please accept our apologies
Пожалуйста, примите наши извинения
pazhalsta, preemeet-ye nashee eezveenyenee-ya

There are good government grants available
Имеются хорошие правительственные дотации
eemye-yootsa kharosheeye praveetyel'stvenniye datatsee

It's a deal
Договорились
dagavareelees'

I'll have to check that with my chairman
Я должен (*m*)/я должна (*f*) обсудить это с моим
председателем
*ya dolzhen/dalzhna absoodeet' eta sma-eem
pryedsyedatyelyem*

I'll get back to you on that
Я обращусь к вам позже по этому вопросу
ya abrashoos' kvam pozhe po etamoo vaprosoo

Our quote will be with you very shortly
Наши расценки вы получите в ближайшее время
nashee rasts_enkee vi pal_oocheet-ye vbleezh_ishye-ye vr_yemya

We'll send it by telex
Мы пошлём это телексом
mi pashl_yom _eta t_yely_eksum

We'll send them airfreight
Мы пошлём это воздушной доставкой
mi pashl_yom _eto vazd_ooshnay dasta_fkay

It's a pleasure to do business with you
Приятно иметь дело с вами
pree-_yatna eem_yet' d_yela sva_mee

We look forward to a mutually beneficial business relationship
Мы ожидаем взаимовыгодного делового сотрудничества
*mi azheeda_-yem vza-eemavigadnava dyelav_ova
satr_oodneechyestva*

RESTAURANTS

The highest standards of service and food are now undoubtedly to be found in the Western-managed hotels and restaurants in the big cities. However, prices tend to be quite high and the dishes generally more oriented to Western cuisine rather than Russian.

There are now a large number of co-operative (private) restaurants and cafés which in general offer good and in some cases excellent standards of both cuisine and service. Prices vary and, from 1st January 1994, you must pay in roubles in all restaurants. Some of the more renowned co-operatives in Moscow include "U Pirosmani" (Georgian), "Skazka", "Glazour" and "Arlecchino", to name but a few. Expect some form of live entertainment here in the evenings, ranging from classical music to topless cabaret. The best way to keep up-to-date with the restaurant scene is to read one of the free English-language newspapers (for instance the Moscow Tribune or Guardian), normally available in hotel foyers.

Finally, there are the state-run restaurants, where in the main standards of service and cuisine have declined in recent years. Their principal attraction now is that most of them are still reasonably priced, meaning it's possible to eat a hearty meal with caviar and champagne without breaking the bank. However, these restaurants remain difficult to book, unless the restaurant in question happens to be in your hotel (as a resident you should assume that you are entitled to dine there).

To avoid disappointment it is always advisable to book your table at least one day in advance, even at the Western-managed restaurants. If you decide to book a table at a state-run restaurant you should start to make arrangements for this well in advance. It's worthwhile too trying to get in at the weekend since this is when the latter are at their more animated.

St. Petersburg justifiably prides itself on better culinary standards than Moscow, making the choice for the consumer wider. As in the West, restaurants' reputations fluctuate and it is always worth asking locals for the most up-to-date recommendations on eating out.

Apart from caviar, vodka (which is ordered by the gram in restaurants) and dry champagne, strongly recommended are the пельмени (*pyelmyenee*), блины (*bleeni*), щи (*shee*), борщ (*borch*) and fresh fish. The best wines come from Georgia and the Crimea and the finest cognac is Armenian.

It is possible to eat very cheaply in more humble establishments, although the food might seem rather basic when compared to the West. The usual rule (as with Russian shops) is simply "what you see is what you get". The café – кафе (*kafe*) is slightly more down-market than the restaurant, and the столовая (*stalova-ya*) is similar to a canteen. Except for the few which smell good and look clean, it is wiser to use these places for cultural rather than culinary purposes (the feathers in your watery chicken soup do at least give a flavour of "eating out" as the average Russian knows it).

Instant snacks are available at a закусочная (*zakoosachna-ya*). A пельменная (*pyel'myenna-ya*) serves meat dumplings and a шашлычная (*shashlichna-ya*) serves spicy meat on a skewer.

The пивной бар (*peevnoy bar*) is like an uninspiring pub; it is generally frequented by men only and is likely to be dirty and overcrowded, and you will probably have to queue up to be served. In return for hard currency, the *valyoota* bars in the larger hotels offer a fair range of alcohol and cigarettes for consumption in surroundings that are always more congenial.

USEFUL WORDS AND PHRASES

beer	пиво	*peeva*
bill	счёт	*shyot*
bottle	бутылка	*bootilka*
bowl	тарелка	*taryelka*
cake	кекс	*kyeks*
caviar	икра	*eekra*

champagne	шампанское	*shampanska-ye*
chef	повар	*povar*
mineral water	минеральная вода	*meenyeral'na-ya vada*
coffee	кофе	*kof-ye*
cup	чашка	*chashka*
fork	вилка	*veelka*
glass	стакан	*stakan*
knife	нож	*nosh*
menu	меню	*myenyoo*
milk	молоко	*malako*
plate	тарелка	*taryelka*
receipt	чек	*chyek*
sandwich	бутерброд	*bootyerbrot*
serviette	салфетка	*salfyetka*
soup	суп	*soop*
spoon	ложка	*loshka*
sugar	сахар	*sakhar*
table	стол	*stol*
tea	чай	*chı*
teaspoon	чайная ложка	*chına-ya loshka*
tip	чаевые	*cha-yeviye*
waiter	официант	*afeetsee-ant*
waitress	официантка	*afeetsee-antka*
water	вода	*vada*
wine	вино	*veeno*

A table for two please
Стол на двоих, пожалуйста
stol na dva-eekh, pazhalsta

But I have ordered a table
Но я заказал (*m*)/заказала (*f*) стол
no ya zakazal/zakazala stol

But those tables are free
Но эти столы свободны
no etee stali svabodni

Can I see the menu?
Можно посмотреть меню?
mozhna pasmatryet' myenyoo?

I would like to book a table for tomorrow evening
Я хочу заказать стол на завтрашний вечер
ya khachoo zakazat' stol na zaftrashnee vyechyer

What would you recommend?
Что вы посоветуете?
shto vi pasavyetoo-yet-ye?

I'd like ...
Я хочу ...
ya khachoo...

100/200 grams of vodka, please
сто/двести граммов водки, пожалуйста
sto/dvyestee gramaf votkee, pazhalsta

Just a cup of coffee, please
Просто чашку кофе, пожалуйста
prosta chashkoo kof-ye, pazhalsta

Waiter!
Товарищ официант!
tavareesh afeetsee-ant!

Can we have the bill, please?
Счёт, пожалуйста
shyot, pazhalsta

RESTAURANTS

I only want a snack
Я хочу только закуску
ya khachoo tol'ka zakooskoo

I didn't order this
Я не заказывал (*m*)/заказывала (*f*) это
ya nye zakazival/zakazivala eta

May we have some more...?
Можно ещё...?
mozhna yeshyo...?

The meal was very good, thank you
Спасибо, было очень вкусно
spaseeba, bila ochyen' fkoosna

YOU MAY HEAR

pree-yatnava apyeteeta
Enjoy your meal

MENU GUIDE

STARTERS

блины с икрой *(bleeni seekroy)*	pancakes with caviar
блины со сметаной *(bleeni sa smyetanay)*	pancakes with sour cream
грибы в сметане *(greebi fsmyetan-ye)*	mushrooms in sour cream
грибы маринованные *(greebi mareenovaniye)*	marinated mushrooms
закуски *(zakooskee)*	starters
заливная рыба *zaleevna-ya riba)*	fish in aspic
икра *(eekra)*	caviar
икра баклажанная *(eekra baklazhana-ya)*	aubergines with onions and tomatoes
икра зернистая *(eekra zyerneesta-ya)*	fresh caviar
икра кетовая *(eekra kyetava-ya)*	red caviar
кильки *(keel'kee)*	sprats
лососина *(lasaseena)*	smoked salmon
осетрина заливная *(asyetreena zaleevna-ya)*	sturgeon in aspic
осетрина с гарниром *(asyetreena zgarneeram)*	sturgeon with garnish
сардины в масле *(sardeeni vmasl-ye)*	sardines in oil
сёмга *(syomga)*	smoked salmon
солёные огурцы *(salyoniye agoortsi)*	pickled cucumbers
солёные помидоры *(salyoniye pameedori)*	pickled tomatoes
фаршированные помидоры *(farsheerovaniye pameedori)*	stuffed tomatoes

SOUPS

борщ *(borsh)*	beef, beetroot and cabbage soup
бульон с пирожками *(bool'yon speerashkamee)*	clear soup with small meat pies
бульон с фрикадельками *(bool'yon sfreekadyel'kamee)*	clear soup with meat balls
мясной бульон *(myasnoy bool'yon)*	clear meat soup
овощной суп *(avashnoy soop)*	vegetable soup

окрошка *(akroshka)* — cold summer soup based on kvas

рассольник *(rasol'neek)* — pickled cucumber soup

солянка *(salyanka)* — spicy soup made from fish or meat and vegetables

суп из свежих грибов *(soop eez svyezheekh greebof)* — fresh mushroom soup

суп картофельный *(soop kartofyel'ni)* — potato soup

суп-лапша с курицей *(soop lapsha skooreetsay)* — chicken noodle soup

суп мясной *(soop myasnoy)* — meat soup

суп томатный *(soop tamatni)* — tomato soup

уха *(ookha)* — fish soup

харчо *(kharcho)* — thick, spicy mutton soup from Georgia

щи *(shee)* — cabbage soup

EGG DISHES

омлет натуральный *(amlyet natooral'ni)* — plain omelette

омлет с ветчиной *(amlyet svyetcheenoy)* — ham omelette

яичница (глазунья) *(ya-eechneetsa glazoon'ya)* — fried eggs

яйца вкрутую *(yitsa fkrootoo-yoo)* — hard-boiled eggs

яйца всмятку *(yitsa fsmyatkoo)* — soft-boiled eggs

яйцо *(yitso)* — egg

яйцо под майонезом *(yitso pod mianyezam)* — egg mayonnaise

FISH

ассорти рыбное *(asartee ribna-ye)* — assorted fish

жареная рыба *(zharyena-ya riba)* — fried fish

камбала *(kambala)* — plaice

карп с грибами *(karp zgreebamee)* — carp with mushrooms

кета *(kyeta)* — Siberian salmon

копчёная сёмга *(kapchyona-ya syomga)* — smoked salmon

осетрина под белым соусом *(asyetreena pod byelim so-oosam)* — sturgeon in white sauce осетрина с гарниром *(asyetreena zgarneeram)* — sturgeon with garnish

осетрина с пикантным соусом *(asyetreena speekantnim so-oosam)* — sturgeon in piquant sauce

осётр запечённый в сметане *(asyotr zapyechyoni fsmyetan-ye)* — sturgeon baked in sour cream

палтус *(paltoos)* — halibut

печень трески в масле *(pyechyen' tryeskee vmasl ye)* — cod liver in oil

рыбные блюда *(ribniye blyooda)* — fish dishes

сельдь *(sye'ld')* — herring

селёдка малосольная *(syelyotka malasol'na-ya)* — slightly salted herring

скумбрия запечённая *(skoombree-ya zapyechyona-ya)* — baked mackerel

судак в белом вине *(soodak vbyelam veen-ye)* — pike-perch in white wine

судак жареный в тесте *(soodak zharyeni ftyest-ye)* — pike-perch fried in batter

судак по-русски *(soodak pa-rooskee)* — pike-perch Russian style

треска *(tryeska)* — cod

тунец *(toonyets)* — tuna fish

фаршированная рыба *(farsheerovana-ya riba)* — stuffed fish

форель *(faryel')* — trout

шпроты *(shproti)* — sprats

щука *(shooka)* — pike

MEAT DISHES

азу *(azoo)* — small pieces of meat in a savoury sauce

ассорти мясное *(asartee myasno-ye)* — assorted meats

битки *(beetkee)* — meat balls

голубцы *(galooptsi)* — cabbage leaves stuffed with meat and rice

дичь *(deech')* — game

колбаса *(kalbasa)* — salami sausage

копчёная колбаса *(kapchyona-ya kalbasa)* — smoked sausage

мясо *(myasa)* — meat

печёнка *(pyechyonka)* — liver

почки *(pochkee)*   kidneys
рубленое мясо *(rooblyena-ye myasa)*   mince meat
рубленые котлеты *(rooblyeniye*   rissoles
  katlyeti)
сосиски *(saseeskee)*   frankfurters
студень *(stoodyen')*   aspic
тефтели с рисом *(tyeftyelee*   small meat balls with rice
  sreesam)
филе *(filyay)*   fillet
шашлык *(shashlik)*   kebab

BEEF

антрекот *(antryekot)*   entrecote steak
беф-строганов *(byef-stroganaf)*   beef Stroganoff
бифштекс натуральный *(beefshtyeks*   fried or grilled beefsteak
  natooral'ni)
говядина отварная с хреном   boiled beef with horseradish
  (gavyadeena atvarna-ya skhryenam)
говядина тушёная *(gavyadeena*   stewed beef
  tooshyona-ya)
гуляш из говядины *(goolyash eez*   beef goulash
  gavyadeeni)
котлеты с грибами *(katlyeti*   steak with mushrooms
  zgreebamee)
рагу из говядины *(ragoo eez*   beef ragout
  gavyadeeni)
ромштекс с луком *(romshtyeks*   minced steak with onion
  slookam)
ростбиф с гарниром *(rostbeef*   cold roast beef with garnish
  zgarneeram)

LAMB

баранина *(baraneena)*   mutton, lamb
бараньи отбивные *(baran'ee*   lamb chops
  atbeevniye)
баранина на вертеле *(baraneena na*   mutton grilled on a skewer
  vyertyel-ye)
битки из баранины *(beetkee eez*   lamb meat balls
  baraneeini)
рагу из баранины *(ragoo eez*   lamb ragout
  baraneeni)

шашлык из баранины *(shashlik eez baraneeni)* lamb kebab

PORK
буженина с гарниром *(boozheneena zgarneerum)* cold boiled pork with garnish

встчина *(vyetcheena)* ham

картофель с ветчиной и шпиком *(kartofyel' svyetcheenoy ee shpeekum)* potatoes with ham and bacon fat

копчёные свиные рёбрышки с фасолью *(kapchoniye sveeniye ryobrishkee sfasol'yoo)* smoked pork ribs with beans

окорок *(okarak)* gammon

свинина жареная с гарниром *(sveeneena zharyena-ya zgarneeram)* fried pork with garnish

свинина с квашеной капустой *(sveeneena skvashenay kapoostay)* pork with sauerkraut

свиные отбивные с чесноком *(sveeniye atbeevniye schyesnakom)* pork chops with garlic

шашлык из свинины с рисом *(shashlik eez sveeneeni sreesam)* pork kebab with rice

VEAL
битки *(beetkee)* meatballs

рулет из рубленой телятины *(roolyet eez rooblyenay tyelyateeni)* minced veal roll

телятина *(tyelyateena)* veal

телячьи отбивные *(tyelyach'ee atbeevniye)* veal chops

фрикадели из телятины в соусе *(freekadyelee eez tyelyateeni fso-oos-ye)* veal meat balls in gravy

шницель с яичницей глазуньей *(shneetsel' sya-eechneetsay glazoon'yay)* schnitzel with fried egg

POULTRY
блюда из птицы *(blyooda eez pteetsi)* poultry dishes

гусь жареный с капустой или яблоками *(goos' zharyeni skapoostay eelee yablakamee)* — roast goose with cabbage or apples

индейка *(indyayka)* — turkey

котлеты по-киевски *(katlyeti pa-kee-yefskee)* — chicken Kiev

пожарские котлеты *(pazharskeeye katlyeti)* — minced chicken

курица *(kooreetsa)* — chicken

отварной цыплёнок *(atvarnoy tsiplyonak)* — boiled chicken

панированный цыплёнок *(paneerovani tsiplyonak)* — chicken in breadcrumbs

птица *(pteetsa)* — poultry

утка *(ootka)* — duck

цыплёнок в тесте *(tsiplyonak ftyest-ye)* — chicken in a pastry

цыплёнок по-охотничьи *(tsiplyonak pa-akhotneech'ee)* — chicken chasseur

цыплёнок «табака» *(tsiplyonak tabaka)* — Caucasian chicken with garlic sauce

цыплёнок фрикасе *(tsiplyonak freekas-ay)* — chicken fricassé

чахохбили *(chakhokhbeelee)* — chicken casserole Georgian style

PIES AND PASTRY DISHES

изделия из теста *(eezdyelee-ya eez tyesta)* — pastry dishes

пельмени *(pyel'myenee)* — meat dumplings

пирог *(peerok)* — pie

пирожки *(peerashkee)* — pies

пирожки с капустой *(peerashkee skapoostay)* — pies filled with cabbage

пирожки с мясом *(peerashkee smyasam)* — pies filled with meat

пирожки с творогом *(peerashkee stvoragam)* — pies filled with cottage cheese

тесто *(tyesta)* — pastry

VEGETABLES

баклажан *(baklazhan)* — aubergine

жареный картофель *(zharyeni kartofyel')*	fried potatoes
зелёный горошек *(zyelyoni garoshek)*	green peas
кабачки *(kabachkee)*	courgettes
капуста *(kapoosta)*	cabbage
картофель *(kartofyel')*	potatoes
кислая капуста *(keesla-ya kapoosta)*	sauerkraut
лук *(look)*	onions, spring onions
морковь *(markof')*	carrots
овощи *(ovashee)*	vegetables
огурец *(agooryets)*	cucumber
перец *(pyeryets)*	pepper
петрушка *(pyetrooshka)*	parsley
помидоры *(pameedori)*	tomatoes
с гарниром *(zgarneeram)*	with garnish
свёкла *(svyokla)*	beetroot
фасоль *(fasol')*	French, haricot or kidney beans
цветная капуста *(tsvyetna-ya kapoosta)*	cauliflower
чеснок *(chyesnok)*	garlic

SALADS

винегрет *(veenyegryet)*	vegetable salad
зелёный салат *(zyelyoni salat)*	green salad
огурцы со сметаной *(agoortsi sa smyetanay)*	cucumber in sour cream
салат «здоровье» *(salat zdarov'ye)*	'health' salad, mixed vegetable salad
салат из лука *(salat eez looka)*	spring onion salad
салат из огурцов *(salat eez agoortsof)*	cucumber salad
салат из помидоров *(salat eez pameedoraf)*	tomato salad
салат из помидоров с брынзой *(salat eez pameedoraf zbrinzay)*	tomato salad with goat's cheese
салат из редиски *(salat eez ryedeeskee)*	radish salad
салат мясной *(salat myasnoy)*	meat salad
салат с крабами *(salat skrabamee)*	crab salad

PASTA AND RICE

вермишель *(vyermeeshel')*	vermicelli
лапша *(lapsha)*	noodles
макароны *(makaroni)*	macaroni
плов *(plof)*	pilaf
рис *(rees)*	rice

BREAD

баранки *(barankee)*	ring-shaped rolls
белый хлеб *(byeli khlyep)*	white bread
бородинский хлеб *(baradeenskee khlyep)*	black rye bread
булки *(boolkee)*	rolls
бутерброд с сыром *(bootyerbrot s-siram)*	cheese sandwich
ржаной хлеб *(rzhanoy khlyep)*	black rye bread
хлеб *(khlyep)*	bread
чёрный хлеб *(chyorni khlyep)*	black bread

CAKES AND DESSERTS

блинчики с вареньем *(bleencheekee svaryen'yem)*	pancakes with jam
блины *(bleeni)*	pancakes
блины со сметаной *(bleeni sa smyetanay)*	pancakes with sour cream
вареник *(varyeneek)*	curd or fruit dumpling
ватрушка *(vatrooshka)*	cheesecake
галушка *(galooshka)*	dumpling
десерт *(dyesyert)*	dessert
желе *(zhelay)*	jelly
кекс *(kyeks)*	fruit cake
кисель *(kisyel')*	thin fruit jelly
кисель из клубники *(keesyel' eez kloobneekee)*	strawberry jelly
кисель из чёрной смородины *(keesyel' eez chyornay smarodeeni)*	blackcurrant jelly
компот из груш *(kampot eez groosh)*	stewed pears
компот из сухофруктов *(kampot eez sookha-frooktaf)*	stewed dried fruit mixture
конфета *(kanfyeta)*	sweet
коржики *(korzheekee)*	flat dry shortbread

крем *(kryem)*	butter cake filling
молочный кисель *(malochni keesyel')*	milk jelly
мороженое клубничное *(marozhena-ye kloobneechna-ye)*	strawberry ice cream
мороженое молочное *(marozhena-ye malochna-ye)*	dairy ice cream
мороженое молочное с ванилином *(marozhena-ye malochna-ye svaneeleenam)*	dairy ice cream with vanilla
мороженое «пломбир» *(marozhena-ye plambeer)*	ice cream with candied fruit
мороженое шоколадное *(marozhena-ye shakaladna-ye)*	chocolate ice cream
печенье *(pyechyen'ye)*	biscuits
пирог с повидлом *(peerok spaveedlam)*	pie with jam
пирог с яблоками *(peerok syablakamee)*	apple pie
пирожное *(peerozhna-ye)*	small cake
повидло *(paveedla)*	thick jelly
пончики *(poncheekee)*	doughnuts
салат из яблок *(salat eez yablak)*	apple salad
сдобное тесто *(zdobna-ye tyesta)*	sweet pastry
сладкое *(slatka-ye)*	dessert, sweet course
сырники *(sirneekee)*	cheesecakes
торт *(tort)*	cake, gateau
фруктовое мороженое *(frooktova-ye marozhena-ye)*	fruit ice cream
шоколад *(shakalat)*	chocolate
эскимо *(eskeemo)*	choc-ice

CHEESE

брынза *(brinza)*	goat's cheese, feta
плавленый сыр *(plavlyeni sir)*	processed cheese
сыр *(sir)*	cheese
творог *(tvorak)*	cottage cheese

FRUIT AND NUTS

абрикосы *(abreekosi)*	apricots
апельсины *(apyel'seeni)*	oranges

MENU GUIDE

арбуз *(arboos)*	water melon
банан *(banan)*	banana
виноград *(veenagrat)*	grapes
грецкий орех *(gryetskee aryekh)*	walnut
груши *(grooshee)*	pears
дыня *(dinya)*	melon
клубника *(kloobneeka)*	strawberries
лимон *(leemon)*	lemon
малина *(maleena)*	raspberries
мандарины *(mandareeni)*	mandarins
орехи *(aryekhee)*	nuts
персик *(pyerseek)*	peach
слива *(sleeva)*	plums
фрукты *(frookti)*	fruit
черешня *(cheryeshnya)*	cherries
чёрная смородина *(chyorna-ya smarodeena)*	blackcurrant
яблоки *(yablakee)*	apples

DRINKS

апельсиновый сок *(apyel'seenavi sok)*	orange juice
белое вино *(byela-ye veeno)*	white wine
вода *(vada)*	water
водка *(votka)*	
газированная вода *(gazeerovana-ya vada)*	soda water
игристое вино *(eegreesto-ye veeno)*	sparkling wine
квас *(kvas)*	kvas (non-alcoholic fizzy drink made of fermented bread and water)
кефир *(kyefeer)*	kefir (sour yogurt drink)
коньяк *(kan'yak)*	brandy
кофе с молоком *(kof-ye smalakom)*	coffee with milk
красное вино *(krasna-ye veeno)*	white wine
минеральная вода *(meenyeral'na-ya vada)*	mineral water
молоко *(malako)*	milk
напитки *(napeetkee)*	drinks

перцовка *(pyertsofka)* — pepper vodka
пиво *(peeva)* — beer
сладкое вино *(slatka-ye veeno)* — dessert wine
томатный сок *(tamatni sok)* — tomato juice
чай *(chı)* — tea
чай с лимоном *(chı sleemonam)* — lemon tea
чёрный кофе *(chyorni kof-ye)* — black coffee
шампанское *(shampanska-ye)* — champagne
яблочный сок *(yablachni sok)* — apple juice

BASIC FOODS

варенье *(varyen'ye)* — jam, preserves
горчица *(garcheetsa)* — mustard
гренки *(gryenkee)* — croutons
гречка *(gryechka)* — buckwheat
джем *(dzhem)* — jam
каша *(kasha)* — buckwheat porridge
маргарин *(margareen)* — margarine
масло *(masla)* — butter, oil
мёд *(myot)* — honey
рассол *(rasol)* — pickle
сливки *(sleefkee)* — cream
сливочное масло *(sleevachna-ye masla)* — butter
сметана *(smyetana)* — sour cream
солёное печенье *(salyona-ye pyechyen'ye)* — savoury biscuit
соль *(sol')* — salt
соус майонез *(so-oos mıanyes)* — mayonnaise sauce
соус хрен *(so-oos khryen)* — horseradish sauce
чёрный перец *(chorni pyeryets)* — black pepper
уксус *(ooksoos)* — vinegar

CULINARY METHODS OF PREPARATION

домашний *(damashnee)* — home-made
жареный *(zharyeni)* — grilled, fried or roast
жареный на вертеле *(zharyeni na vyertyel-ye)* — grilled on a skewer
отварной *(atvarnoy)* — boiled, poached
печёный *(pyechyoni)* — baked

сырой *(siroy)*	raw
тушёный *(tooshyoni)*	stewed
фаршированный *(farsheerovani)*	stuffed

MENU TERMS

блюдо *(blyooda)*	dish, course
меню *(myenyoo)*	menu
национальные русские блюда *(natseeanal'niye rooskeeye blyooda)*	Russian national dishes
основное блюдо *(asnavna-ye blyoodo)*	main course
первое блюдо *(pyerva-ye blyoodo)*	first course
русская кухня *(rooska-ya kookhnya)*	Russian cuisine
фирменные блюда *(feermyeniye blyooda*	specialty dishes

SHOPPING

If you are looking for presents to take home, then one option is to visit a Берёзка (*beryozka*) shop which sells souvenirs, alcohol and tobacco. The most attractive goods are blue and white Gzhel crockery, hand-painted trays, lacquered miniature boxes and brooches from Palekh, matryoshka dolls, jewellery and pretty head scarves. From 1st January 1994, payment in these shops, as in all others, can be made only in roubles. Your hard currency can be easily changed at any of the numerous exchange points, some of which are located in the shops themselves.

However, by far the widest selection of traditional Russian souvenirs and the best bargains are to be found in street art markets such as the one on the Арбат (*arbat*), or at Вернисаж (*vyerneesazh*) in Moscow. Quality and prices vary, but haggling is acceptable practice here. Payment is normally possible in either roubles or hard currency but you should check the current exchange rates beforehand, to avoid being shortchanged. It is not recommended that food such as caviar be bought here since it may not always be the genuine article.

Two shopping malls well worth a visit are ГУМ (goom; the letters stand for "State Universal Shop") opposite the Kremlin, and Петровский Пассаж (*petrovskee passazh*), just a couple of minutes walk from the Bolshoi Theatre.

Another shop which should not be left off your itinerary is "Елисеевский" (*yeleesye-evskee*) food shop, on Moscow's Tverskaya Street, and its twin on St. Petersburg's Nevsky Prospekt. Despite being rather neglected by time both shops remain striking examples of Russia's pre-revolutionary style.

More ambitious shoppers may be delighted to discover that works of art and antiques can sometimes be sold very unceremoniously and at relatively low prices. Before you buy, make enquiries to ensure you will not be disappointed as, without a receipt from a *beryozka* or official permission from the Ministry of Culture to take any "work of art" out of the country, there is a risk the item will be confiscated from you at the airport.

USEFUL WORDS AND PHRASES

baker	булочная	*boolachna-ya*
butcher	мясо (*literally meat*)	*myasa*
bookshop	книжный магазин	*kneezhni magazeen*
bookshop (*second-hand*)	букинистический магазин	*bookeeneesteechy-eskee magazeen*
to buy	купить	*koopeet'*
cake shop	кондитерская	*kandeetyerska-ya*
cheap	дешёвый/ дешёвая/ дешёвое	*dyeshyovi/ dyeshyova-ya/ dyeshyova-ye*
chemist	аптека	*aptyeka*
department store	универмаг	*ooneevyermak*
fashion	мода	*moda*
fishmonger	рыба (*literally fish*)	*riba*
florist	цветы (*literally flowers*)	*tsvyeti*
foodstore	гастроном	*gastranom*
grocer	бакалея (*literally groceries*)	*bakalye-ya*
ladies' wear	женская одежда	*zhenska-ya adyezhda*
market	рынок	*rinak*
menswear	мужская одежда	*mooshska-ya adyezhda*
newspaper kiosk	газетный киоск	*gazyetni kee-osk*
receipt	чек	*chyek*
record shop	грампластинки (*literally records*)	*gramplasteenkee*
shoe repairs	ремонт обуви	*ryemont oboovee*
shoe shop	обувь (*literally footwear*)	*oboof'*
shop	магазин	*magazeen*

to go shopping	ходить по магазинам	*khadeet' po magazeenam*
souvenir shop	сувениры (*literally souvenirs*)	*soovyeneeri*
to spend	тратить	*trateet'*
stationer	канцтовары	*kantstavari*
supermarket	универсам	*ooneevyersam*
till	касса	*kasa*
toyshop	игрушки (*literally toys*)	*eegrooshkee*

I'd like...
Я хочу...
ya khachoo...

Do you have...?
У вас ест...?
oo vas yest'...?

How much is this?
Сколько это стоит?
skol'ka eta sto-eet?

Where is the... department?
Где отдел...?
gdye atdyel...?

Do you have any more of these?
У вас есть ещё?
oo vas yest' yeshyo?

I'd like to change this please
Будьте добры, я хочу это поменять
boo't-ye dabri, ya khachoo eta pamyenyat'

Have you anything cheaper?
У вас есть что-нибудь дешевле?
oo vas yest' shto-neeboot' dyeshevl-ye?

Have you anything larger?
У вас есть побольше?
oo vas yest' pabol'she?

Have you anything smaller?
У вас есть поменьше?
oo vas yest' pamyen'she?

Do you have it in other colours?
У вас есть другого цвета?
oo vas yest' droogova tsvyeta?

Could you wrap it for me, please?
Заверните, пожалуйста
zavyerneet-ye, pazhalsta

Can I have a receipt?
Дайте, пожалуйста чек
dIt-ye, pazhalsta chyek

Can I have a bag please?
Дайте, пожалуйста пакет
dIt-ye, pazhalsta pakyet

Can I try it/them on?
Можно померять?
mozhna pamyeryat'?

Where do I pay?
Куда платить?
kooda plateet'?

Can I have a refund?
Я хочу получить обратно деньги
ya khachoo paloocheet' abratna dyen'gee

I'm just looking
Я просто смотрю
ya prosta smatryoo

I'll come back later
Я вернусь позже
ya vyernoos' pozhe

THINGS YOU'LL SEE

бакалея *bakalye-ya*	groceries
букинистический магазин *bookeeneesteechyeskee magazeen*	second-hand bookshop
булочная *boolachna-ya*	bakery
бытовая химия *bitova-ya kheemee-ya*	household cleaning materials
верхний этаж *vyerkhnee etash*	upper floor
возьмите тележку/корзину *vaz'meet-ye tyelyeshkoo/ karzeenoo*	please take a trolley/basket
женская одежда *zhenska-ya adyezhda*	ladies' clothing
игрушки *eegrooshkee*	toys
канцтовары *kantstavari*	stationer
касса *kasa*	cash desk, till
книги *kneegee*	bookshop
количество *kaleechyestva*	quantity
кондитерская *kandeetyerska-ya*	cake shop
меха *myekha*	fur shop
мода *moda*	fashion
мороженое *marozhena-ye*	ice cream shop

→

мужская одежда	*mooshska-ya adyezhda*	menswear
мясо	*myasa*	butcher
не трогать	*nye trogat'*	please do not touch
обувь	*oboof'*	shoe shop
овощи	*ovashee*	vegetables
отдел	*atdyel*	department
первый этаж	*pyervi etash*	ground floor
прокат	*prakat*	rental
самообслуживание	*sama-absloozheevaneeye*	self-service
табак	*tabak*	tobacconist
универмаг	*ooneevyermak*	department store
цветы	*tsvyeti*	flowers
цена	*tsyena*	price

THINGS YOU'LL HEAR

oo vas yest' myelach'?
Have you any smaller money?

eezveeneet-ye, oo nas etava paka nyet
Sorry, we're out of stock

eta fsyo, shto oo nas yest'
This is all we have

shto-neeboot' yeshyo?
Will there be anything else?

AT THE HAIRDRESSER

USEFUL WORDS AND PHRASES

appointment	запись	*zapees'*
beard	борода	*barada*
blond man/woman	блондин/ блондинка	*blandeen/ blandeenka*
brush	щётка	*shyotka*
comb	расчёска	*raschyoska*
curlers	бигуди	*beegoodee*
curly	кудрявый	*koodryavi*
dark	тёмный	*tyomni*
fringe	чёлка	*chyolka*
gel	желе для волос	*zhelay dlya valos*
hair	волосы	*volasi*
haircut	стрижка	*streeshka*
hairdresser	парикмахер	*pareekhmakhyer*
hairdryer	фен	*fyen*
hairspray	лак для волос	*lak dlya valos*
long hair	длинные волосы	*dleeniye volasi*
moustache	усы	*oosi*
parting	пробор	*prabor*
perm	перманент	*pyermanyent*
shampoo	шампунь	*shampoon'*
shaving foam	крем для бритья	*kryem dlya breet'ya*
short hair	короткие волосы	*karotkeeye volasi*
wavy hair	вьющиеся волосы	*v'yooshee-yesya volasi*

AT THE HAIRDRESSER

I'd like to make an appointment
Я хочу записаться
ya khachoo zapeesat'sa

Just a trim please
Немного подстрегите, пожалуйста
nyemnoga padstryegeet-ye, pazhalsta

Not too much off
Много не снимайте
mnoga nye sneemIt-ye

A bit more off here please
Покороче здесь, пожалуйста
pakaroch-ye zdyes', pazhalsta

I'd like a cut and blow-dry
Подстригите и сделайте укладку феном
padstreegeet-ye ee zdyelIt-ye ooklatkoo fyenam

I'd like a perm
Я хочу перманент
ya khachoo pyermanyent

I don't want any hairspray
Лака не нужно
laka nye noozhna

THINGS YOU'LL SEE

женский зал	*zhenskee zal*	ladies' salon
краска для волос	*kraska dlya valos*	tint
мастер	*mastyer*	hairdresser

→

мужской зал	*mooshskoy zal*	men's hairdresser
парикмахер	*pareekmakyer*	hairdresser
парикмахерская	*pareekmakherska-ya*	hairdresser's
перманент	*pyermanyent*	perm
сухой	*sookhoy*	dry
укладка	*ooklatka*	set
уложить волосы феном	*oolazheet' volasi fyenam*	to blow dry

THINGS YOU'LL HEAR

shto vi khateet-ye?
How would you like it?

eta dastatachna koratka?
Is that short enough?

pakrit' lakam?
Would you like any hair-spray?

SPORT

Active involvement by tourists in sport in Russia is most likely to mean swimming, skating or skiing. Ask your hotel information service for details of how and where to do what you want. Cross-country skiing is popular and skis for this may be hired (e.g. at Sokolneekee Park in Moscow) or even bought with relative ease. If you go anywhere off the beaten track, make sure that you are with local people who know what they are doing. Down-hill skiing is becoming a popular tourist attraction in the Caucasus, but skiers should not expect to find it like Verbiers or Val d'Isère. You should check well in advance with the tour organiser on what you may need to bring yourself, rather than assume that skiing equipment will be available on site.

The Black Sea resorts are excellent for swimming, and swimming pools can be found in Moscow, St. Petersburg and the larger towns. The large outdoor pool opposite the Pushkin Museum of Fine Arts on Kropotkeenskaya in Moscow is heated all year round, and enables the more hardy to swim outdoors irrespective of the temperature.

Full details of current sporting events for spectators can be obtained by asking your hotel information desk or Intourist. Sportsmen and women undertaking any activity outdoors in a Russian winter should be very wary of the cold. It can be ferocious and, if you stop feeling the cold through what may initially seem like a welcome loss of sensation (rather than by generating your own body heat), get inside quickly – it is the first symptom of frost-bite.

USEFUL WORDS AND PHRASES

athletics	атлетика	*atlyeteeka*
badminton	бадминтон	*badmeenton*
ball	мяч	*myach*
beach	пляж	*plyash*
bicycle	велосипед	*vyelaseepyet*

canoe	каноэ	*kanoe*
chess	шахматы	*shakhmati*
cross-country skiing	лыжный спорт	*lizhni sport*
cross-country skis	лыжи	*lizhee*
deckchair	шезлонг	*shezlonk*
downhill skiing	горнолыжный спорт	*garna-lizhni sport*
downhill skis	горные лыжи	*gorniye lizhee*
fishing	рыболовство	*ribalofstva*
fishing rod	удочка	*oodachka*
flippers	ласты	*lasti*
football (*sport*)	футбол	*footbol*
football (*ball*)	футбольный мяч	*footbol'ni myach*
football match	футбольный матч	*footbol'ni match*
goggles	защитные очки	*zasheetniye achkee*
gymnastics	гимнастика	*geemnasteeka*
harpoon	гарпун	*garpoon*
hockey	хоккей	*khakay*
jogging	бег трусцой	*byek troostsoy*
lake	озеро	*ozyera*
lifebelt	спасательный пояс	*spasatyel'ni po-yas*
lifeguard	спасатель	*spasatyel'*
mountaineering	альпинизм	*al'peeneezm*
oxygen bottles	кислородные баллоны	*keeslarodniye baloni*
pedal boat	водный велосипед	*vodni vyelaseepyet*
racket	ракетка	*rakyetka*
riding	верховая езда	*vyerkhava-ya yezda*
rowing boat	вёсельная лодка	*vyosyel'na-ya lotka*
to run	бегать	*byegat'*
sailing	парусный спорт	*paroosni sport*
sand	песок	*pyesok*
sea	море	*mor-ye*

83

to skate	кататься на коньках	*katat'sa na kan'kakh*
skates	коньки	*kan'kee*
skating rink	каток	*katok*
to ski	кататься на лыжах	*katat'sa na lizhakh*
skin diving	подводное плавание	*padvodna-ye plavaneeye*
stadium	стадион	*stadee-on*
sunshade	солнечный зонт	*solnyechni zont*
to swim	плавать	*plavat'*
swimming pool	бассейн	*basyayn*
table tennis	настольный теннис	*nastol'ni tyenees*
tennis	теннис	*tyenees*
tennis court	теннисный корт	*tyeneesni kort*
tennis racket	теннисная ракетка	*tyeneesna-ya rakyetka*
volleyball	волейбол	*valyaybol*
walking	ходьба	*khad'ba*
water skiing	воднолыжный спорт	*vadna-lizhni sport*
water skis	водные лыжи	*vodniye lizhee*
wave	волна	*valna*
wet suit	плавательный костюм	*plavatyel'ni kastyoom*
windsurfing board	доска для серфинга	*daska dlya syerfeenga*
yacht	яхта	*yakhta*

How do I get to the beach?
Как попасть на пляж?
kak papast' na plyash?

How deep is the water here?
Какая глубина воды здесь?
kaka-ya gloobeena vadi zdyes'?

Is there an outdoor pool here?
Здесь есть открытый бассейн?
zdyes' yest' atkriti basyayn?

Can one swim here?
Здесь можно плавать?
zdyes' mozhna plavat'?

Can I fish here?
Здесь можно ловить рыбу?
zdyes' mozhna laveet' riby?

Do I need a licence?
Мне нужно разрешение?
mnye noozhna razryesheneeye?

I would like to hire a sunshade
Можно взять напрокат зонтик?
mozhna vzyat' naprakat zonteek?

How much does it cost per hour?
Сколько это стоит в час?
skol'ka eta sto-eet fchas?

I would like to take water-skiing lessons
Я хочу брать уроки по водным лыжам
ya khachoo brat' oorokee pa vodnim lizham

Where can I hire...?
Где можно взять напрокат...?
gdye mozhna vzyat' naprakat...?

THINGS YOU'LL SEE

билеты *beelyeti*	tickets
велосипедная трасса *vyelaseepyedna-ya trasa*	cycle path
велосипеды *vyelaseepyedi*	bicycles
водные виды спорта *vodniye veedi sporta*	water sports
горные лыжи *gorniye lizhee*	downhill skis
коньки *kan'kee*	skates
лыжи *lizhee*	cross-country skis
напрокат *naprakat*	for hire
не прыгать *nye prigat'*	no diving
парусные лодки *paroosniye lotkee*	sailing boats
первая помощь *pyerva-ya pomash'*	first aid
плавать запрещается *plavat' zapryesha-yetsa*	no swimming
пляж *plyash*	beach
порт *port*	port
рыбная ловля запрещена *ribna-ya lovlya zapryeshena*	no fishing
спортивное оборудование *sparteevna-ye abaroodeevaneeye*	sporting facilities
спортивный центр *sparteevni tsyentr*	sports centre
спасательный пояс *spasatyel'ni po-yas*	lifebelt
спасатель *spasatel'*	lifeguard
стадион *stadee-on*	stadium
уроки по водным лыжам *oorokee pa vodnim lizham*	water-skiing lessons
футбольное поле *footbol'na-ye pol-ye*	football pitch

POST OFFICES AND BANKS

As far as postage is concerned, it is easier to use the facilities at your hotel, if these are available, rather than go to a post office. You will thus avoid long queues and will be able to deal with people who are used to foreigners. You will not have to suffer the more exasperating features of the postal service, such as arbitrary closing or having no stamps. For airmail letters use a международный конверт (*mezhdoonarodni kanvyert*) or international envelope, and allow an average of two weeks for arrival. Postcards, stamps and envelopes can be purchased at newspaper kiosks and post offices. Mail boxes are blue; in Moscow, those painted red are for local (city) mail only.

Most large towns and cities now boast a multitude of exchange bureaux and banks where you can change hard currency for roubles and vice versa — rates do not usually vary sufficiently from bank to bank to merit shopping around. Successive devaluations of the rouble since 1989 have led to an astronomic increase in the number of roubles to the pound. This, among other things, has had the effect of all but eliminating the attraction of the black market, where you still run the distinct risk of being landed with a wad of forgeries in return for your hard currency.

Although customs currency checks have relaxed in recent years it's still advisable to get and retain exchange receipts to account for expenditure of the currency you will have declared on your currency declaration form when you entered the country.

It should be noted that the rouble is now the only legal form of tender in Russian shops and restaurants. Hard currency is no longer accepted in its cash form although a growing number of outlets do take credit cards. Your hard currency can be easily changed at exchange points, some of which will be located in the shops themselves. Rates offered in the latter, however, tend to be worse than "outside", in the banks and independent exchange bureaux.

USEFUL WORDS AND PHRASES

airmail	авиапочта	*avee-apochta*
bank	банк	*bank*
banknote	банкнота	*banknota*
to change	обменять	*abmyenyat'*
cheque	чек	*chyek*
collection	выемка	*vi-yemka*
counter	стойка	*stoyka*
customs form	таможенная	*tamozhena-ya*
	декларация	*dyeklaratsee-ya*
delivery	поставка	*pastafka*
dollar	доллар	*dolar*
exchange rate	обменный курс	*abmyeni koors*
form	бланк	*blank*
international money	заказ на	*zakas na*
order	международный	*myezhdoo-*
	перевод	*narodni*
		pyeryevot
letter	письмо	*pees'mo*
letter box	почтовый ящик	*pachtovi yasheek*
parcel	посылка	*pasilka*
post	почта	*pochta*
postage rates	почтовые тарифы	*pachtoviye tareefi*
postcard	открытка	*atkritka*
postcode	почтовый индекс	*pachtovi eendyeks*
poste-restante	почта до	*pochta da*
	востребования	*vastryebavanee-*
		ya
postman	почтальон	*pachtal'on*
post office	почта	*pochta*
pound sterling	фунт стерлингов	*foont styerleengaf*
registered letter	заказное письмо	*zakazno-ye*
		pees'mo
stamp	марка	*marka*
telegram	телеграмма	*tyelyegrama*
traveller's cheque	дорожный чек	*darozhni chyek*

How much is a postcard to...?
Сколько стоит открытка в...?
skol'ka sto-eet atkritka v...?

I want to register this letter
Я хочу отправить заказное письмо
ya khachoo atpraveet' zakazno-ye pees'mo

I want to send this this letter to...
Я хочу отправить это письмо в...
ya khachoo atpraveet' eta pees'mo v...

By airmail, please
Авиапочтой, пожалуйста
avee-apochtay, pazhalsta

How long does the post to... take?
Сколько это будет идти до...?
skol'ka eta boodyet eetee do...?

Where can I post this?
Где я могу это отправить?
gdye ya magoo eta atpraveet'?

Is there any mail for me?
Есть письма для меня?
yest' pees'ma dlya myenya?

My surname is...
Моя фамилия...
ma-ya fameelee-ya...

I'd like to send a telegram
Я хочу отправить телеграмму
ya khachoo atpraveet' tyelyegramoo

POST OFFICES AND BANKS

I'd like to change this into...
Я хочу разменять это на...
ya khachoo razmyenyat' eta na...

Can I cash these traveller's cheques?
Можно обменять эти дорожные чеки?
mozhna abmyenyat' etee darozhniye chyekee?

What is the exchange rate for the pound/dollar?
Какой курс обмена фунтов стерлингов/долларов?
kakoy koors abmyena foontaf styerleengaf/dolaraf?

THINGS YOU'LL SEE

авиапочта	*avee-apochta*	airmail
адрес	*adryes*	address
адресат	*adryesat*	addressee
банк	*bank*	bank
денежные переводы	*dyenyezhniye pyeryevodi*	money orders
заказные письма	*zakazniye pees'ma*	registered mail
заполнить	*zapolneet'*	to fill in
касса	*kasa*	cashdesk
марка	*marka*	stamp
марки	*markee*	stamps
обмен валюты	*abmyen valyooti*	currency exchange
открытка	*atkritka*	postcard
отправитель	*atpraveetyel'*	sender
пакет	*pakyet*	packet
письмо	*pees'mo*	letter
почта	*pochta*	letterbox; post office

→

почта до востребования *pochta da vastryebavanee-ya*	poste-restante
почтовый индекс *pachtovi eendyeks*	post code
приём посылок *pree-yom pasilak*	parcels counter
стоимость международной отправки *sto-eemast' myezhdoo-narodnay atprafkee*	postage abroad
тариф *tareef*	charge
телеграммы *tyelyegrami*	telegrams
часы работы *chasi raboti*	opening hours

TELEPHONES

You should be able to make both international and local calls from your hotel.

The majority of hotels in the big cities now have international phone booths or satellite phone facilities. These booths take phonecards which can normally be bought from your hotel reception, as well as several major credit cards. If you do not have access to an international direct-dial phone, then your call must be booked through the operator.

To avoid delay, international calls should be booked well in advance. Although essential phrases are included below, the operators connecting you will normally speak English. If unable to call from a hotel, you can as a last option go to a telephone and telegraph office to make the call from there.

USEFUL WORDS AND PHRASES

call	звонок	*zvanok*
to call	звонить	*zvaneet'*
code	код	*kot*
to dial	набирать номер	*nabeerat' nomyer*
dialling tone	гудок	*goodok*
fire	пожар (01)	*pazhar*
police	милиция (02)	*meeleetsee-ya*
ambulance	скорая помощь (03)	*skora-ya pomash'*
enquiries	справочная (09)	*spravachna-ya*
extension (number)	добавочный (номер)	*dabavachni (nomyer)*
international call	международный звонок	*myezhdoo-narodni zvanok*
number	номер	*nomyer*
pay-phone	телефон-автомат	*tyelyefon-aftamat*

receiver	(телефонная) трубка	*(tyelyefona-ya) troopka*
telephone	телефон	*tyelyefon*
telephone box	телефон-автомат	*tyelyefon-aftamat*
telephone directory	телефонный справочник	*tyelyefoni spravachneek*
wrong number	неправильный номер	*nyepraveel'ni notyer*

Where is the nearest phone box?
Где ближайший телефон-автомат?
gdye bleezhIshee tyelyefon-aftamat?

Is there a telephone directory?
У вас есть телефонный справочник?
oo vas yest' tyelyefoni spravachneek?

I would like the directory for...
Мне нужен телефонный справочник для...
mnye noozhen tyelyefoni spravachneek dlya...

I would like to order a call to London for 8 o'clock tomorrow evening
Я хочу заказать разговор с Лондоном на восемь вечера завтра
ya khachoo zakazat' razgavor slondanam na vosyem' vyechyera zaftra

Can I call abroad from here?
Можно позвонить заграницу отсюда?
mozhna pazvaneet' zagraneetsoo atsyooda?

How much is a call to...?
Сколько стоит звонок в...?
skol'ka sto-eet zvanok v...?

TELEPHONES

I would like a number in...
Мне нужен номер в...
mnye noozhen nomyer v...

Hello, this is... speaking
Алло, говорит...
allo, gavareet...

Is that...?
это...?
eta...?

Speaking (*literally: I'm listening*)
Слушаю
sloosha-yoo

I would like to speak to...
Позовите, пожалуйста...
pazaveet-ye, pazhalsta...

Extension..., please
Добавочный..., пожалуйста
dabavachni..., pazhalsta

Please say that he/she called
Пожалуйста, передайте, что звонил (*m*)/звонила (*f*)
pazhalsta, pyeryedit-ye shto zvaneel/zvaneela

Ask him/her to call me back, please
Попросите его/её позвонить мне, пожалуйста
papraseet-ye yevo/yeyo pazvaneet' mnye, pazhalsta

My number is...
Мой номер...
moy nomyer...

Do you know where he/she is?
Вы знаете, где он/она?
vi zna-yet-ye gdye on/ana?

When will he/she be back?
Когда он/она вернётся?
kagda on/ana vyernyotsa?

Could you leave him/her a message?
Вы можете передать ему/ей?
vi mozhet-ye pyeryedat' yemoo/yay?

I'll ring back later
Я позвоню позже
ya pazvanyoo pozhe

Sorry, wrong number
Вы не туда попали
vi nye tooda papalee

THINGS YOU'LL SEE

код *kot*	code
междугородный звонок *myezhdoo-garodni zvanok*	long-distance call
международный звонок *myezhdoo-narodni zvanok*	international call
местный звонок *myestni zvanok*	local call
милиция *meeleetsee-ya*	police
не работает *nye rabota-yet*	out of order
пожар *pazhar*	fire
прямой номер *pryamoy nomyer*	direct dialling
скорая помощь *skora-ya pomash'*	ambulance
справочная *spravachna-ya*	enquiries

→

стоимость *sto-eemast'*		charges
телефон *tyelyefon*		telephone
телефон-автомат *tyelyefon-aftamat*		telephone box/ pay-phone

---

REPLIES YOU MAY BE GIVEN

skyem vi khateet-ye gavareet'?
Who would you like to speak to?

vi nye tooda papalee
You've got the wrong number

kto gavareet?
Who's speaking?

allo
Hello

kakoy oo vas nomyer?
What is your number?

eezveeneet-ye, yevo/ye-yo nyet
Sorry, he/she's not in

on/ana vyernyotsa v...
He/she'll be back at... o'clock

pyeryezvaneet-ye, pazhalsta, zaftra
Please call again tomorrow

ya pyeryedam shto vi zvaneelee
I'll say that you called

HEALTH

If you fall seriously ill during your visit to Russia, notify the hotel management and Intourist that you need both medical attention and an interpreter. Sometimes, the Russian doctor treating you will have a good command of English but, wherever possible, it is worth making arrangements for an interpreter immediately so as to ensure that (in all cases of serious illness) mutual comprehension is established between doctor and patient without wasting any time.

Medical attention is free for all illnesses which travellers contract while in Russia. Travellers feeling the onset of a serious illness may prefer to travel home immediately, if this is possible. This is because, despite the excellent standards which prevail amongst the medical profession, Russian medical technology is not the most advanced in the world. If you or someone under your care needs to fly home urgently, it is always worth checking that all requirements have been fulfilled for making insurance claims at a later date (e.g. obtaining doctor's certificates, with details of names, dates and illnesses etc).

In less urgent cases of illness you should, with the help of the phrases and vocabulary below, be able to fend for yourself.

USEFUL WORDS AND PHRASES

accident	несчастный случай	*nyeshastni sloochı*
ambulance	скорая помощь	*skora-ya pomash'*
appendicitis	апендицит	*apyendeetseet*
appendix	апендикс	*apyendeeks*
aspirin	аспирин	*aspeereen*
asthma	астма	*astma*
backache	боль в спине	*bol' fspeen-ye*
bandage	бинт	*beent*

bite (*by dog*)	укус (собаки)	*ookoos (sabakee)*
bite (*by insect*)	укус (насекомого)	*ookoos (nasyekomava)*
bladder	мочевой пузырь	*machyevoy poozir'*
blister	волдырь	*valdir'*
blood	кровь	*krof'*
burn (*noun*)	ожог	*azhok*
cancer	рак	*rak*
chemist	аптека	*aptyeka*
chest	грудь	*groot'*
chickenpox	ветрянка	*vyetryanka*
cold (*noun*)	простуда	*prastooda*
concussion	контузия	*kantoozee-ya*
constipation	запор	*zapor*
contact lenses	контактные линзы	*kantaktniye leenzi*
corn	мозоль	*mazol'*
cough (*noun*)	кашель	*kashel'*
cut	порез	*paryes*
dentist	зубной врач	*zoobnoy vrach*
diabetes	диабет	*dee-abyet*
diarrhoea	понос	*panos*
dizziness	головокружение	*galava-kroozheneeye*
doctor (*profession*)	врач	*vrach*
doctor (*as form of address*)	доктор	*doktar*
earache	боль в ухе	*bol' vookh-ye*
fever	температура	*tyempyeratoora*
filling	пломба	*plomba*
first aid	первая помощь	*pyerva-ya pomash'*
flu	грипп	*greep*
fracture	перелом	*pyeryelom*
German measles	краснуха	*krasnookha*
glasses	очки	*achkee*
gum	десна	*dyesna*
haemorrhage	кровотечение	*kravatyechyeneeye*
hayfever	сенная лихорадка	*syenna-ya leekharatka*

headache	головная боль	*galavna-ya bol'*
heart	сердце	*syertse*
heart attack	сердечный	*syerdyechni*
	приступ	*preestoop*
hospital	больница	*bal'neetsa*
ill	болен (*m*)/	*bolyen/bal'na*
	больна (*f*)	
indigestion	несварение	*nyesvaryeneeye*
infected	заражённый	*zarazhyoni*
injection	укол	*ookol*
itch	зуд	*zoot*
kidney	почка	*pochka*
lump	опухоль	*opookhal'*
measles	корь	*kor'*
migraine	мигрень	*meegryen'*
mumps	свинка	*sveenka*
nausea	тошнота	*tashnata*
nurse	медсестра	*myedsyestra*
operation	операция	*apyeratsee-ya*
optician	окулист	*akooleest*
pain	боль	*bol'*
penicillin	пенициллин	*pyeneetseeleen*
plaster (*sticky*)	пластырь	*plastir'*
plaster (*of Paris*)	гипс	*geeps*
pneumonia	пневмония	*pnyevmanee-ya*
pregnant	беременная	*byeryemyena-ya*
prescription	рецепт	*ryetsept*
rheumatism	ревматизм	*ryevmateezm*
scratch	царапина	*tsarapeena*
sore throat	боль в горле	*bol' vgorl-ye*
splinter	заноза	*zanoza*
sprain	растяжение	*rastyazheneeye*
	связок	*svyazak*
sting	укус	*ookoos*
stomach	желудок	*zheloodak*
temperature	температура	*tyempyeratoora*
tonsils	миндалины	*meendaleeni*

99

toothache	зубная боль	*zoobna-ya bol'*
ulcer	язва	*yazva*
vaccination	прививка	*preeveefka*
whooping cough	коклюш	*kaklyoosh*

I feel sick
меня тошнит
myenya tashneet

I feel travel sick
меня укачало
myenya ookachala

I have a pain in...
У меня болит...
oo myenya baleet...

I do not feel well
Мне плохо
mnye plokha

I feel faint
Мне дурно
mnye doorna

I feel dizzy
У меня кружится голова
oo myenya kroozheetsa galava

It hurts here
Болит здесь
baleet zdyes'

It's a sharp pain
Острая боль
ostra-ya bol'

It's a dull pain
Тупая боль
toopa-ya bol'

It hurts all the time
Болит всё время
baleet fsyo vryemya

It only hurts now and then
Болит время от времени
baleet vryema at vryemyenee

It hurts when you touch it
Болит, когда вы трогаете
baleet kagda vi troga-yet-ye

It hurts more at night
Болит сильнее ночью
baleet seel'nye-ye noch'yoo

It stings
Жжёт
zhyot

It aches
Болит
baleet

I have a temperature
У меня температура
oo myenya tyetpyeratoora

I need a prescription for...
Мне нужен рецепт для...
mnye noozhen ryetsept dlya...

I normally take...
Обычно я принимаю...
abichna ya preeneema-yoo...

I'm allergic to...
У меня аллергия на...
oo myenya allyergee-ya na...

Have you got anything for...?
У вас есть что-нибудь от...?
oo vas yest' shto-neeboot' ot...?

Do I need a prescription for this?
Мне нужен рецепт для этого?
mnye noozhen ryetsept dlya etava?

I have lost a filling
У меня выпала пломба
oo myenya vipala plomba

THINGS YOU'LL SEE

больница *bal'neetsa*	hospital
врач *vrach*	doctor
дежурная аптека *dyezhoorna-ya aptyeka*	duty chemist
зубной врач *zoobnoy vrach*	dentist
клиника *kleeneeka*	clinic
кровяное давление *kravyano-ye davlyeneeye*	blood pressure
лекарство *lyekarstva*	medicine
нарыв *nariv*	abscess
натощак *natashak*	on an empty stomach
окулист *akooleest*	optician
осмотр *asmotr*	check-up
отолоринголог *atalareengolak*	ear, nose and throat specialist
очки *achkee*	glasses
пломба *plomba*	filling
поликлиника *paleekleeneeka*	surgery
пункт скорой помощи *poonkt skoray pomashee*	First Aid Post
рентген *ryentgyen*	X-ray
рецепт *ryetsept*	prescription
скорая помощь *skora-ya pomash'*	ambulance
укол *ookol*	injection

THINGS YOU'LL HEAR

preeneemIt-ye po... tablyetkee
Take... tablets at a time

svadoy
With water

razhooyt-ye
Chew them

adeen raz/dva raza/tree raza vdyen'
Once/twice/three times a day

tol'ka pyeryed snom
Only when you go to bed

shto vi abichna preeneema-yet-ye?
What do you normally take?

vam noozhna pItee kvrachoo
I think you should see a doctor

eezveeneet-ye, oo nas etava nyet
I'm sorry, we don't have that

dlya etava vam noozhen ryetsept
For that you need a prescription

MINI-DICTIONARY

about: about 16 okala
  shesnatsatee
accident avaree-ya
accommodation razmyesheneeye
ache bol'
adaptor transfarmatar
address adryes
after posl-ye
after-shave adyekalon
again snova
against proteef
air-conditioning kandeetsee-anyer
aircraft samalyot
air hostess styoo-ardyesa
airline avee-aleenee-ya
airport aeraport
alarm clock boodeel'neek
alcohol alkagol'
all vyes'
  all the streets fsye ooleetsi
  that's all, thanks fsyo, spaseeba
almost pachtee
alone adeen
already oozhe
always fsyegda
ambulance skora-ya pomash'
America amyereeka
American amyereekanskee
  (man) amyereekanyets
  (woman) amyereekanka
and ee
ankle ladishka
anorak koortka
another: another room droogoy
  nomyer
  another coffee yeshyo kof-ye
anti-freeze anteefrees
antique shop anteekvarni
  magazeen

apartment kvarteera
aperitif apyereeteef
appetite apyeteet
apple yablaka
application form blank
appointment zapees'
apricot abreekos
arm rooka
art eeskoostva
art gallery khoodozhestvyena-ya
  galyerye-ya
artist khoodozhneek
as: as soon as possible kak
  mozhna skarye-ye
ashtray pyepyel'neetsa
aspirin aspeereen
at: at the post office na pocht-ye
  at night noch'yoo
  at 3 o'clock ftree chasa
attractive preevlyekatyel'ni
aunt tyotya
Australia afstralee-ya
Australian afstraleeskee
  (man) afstrale-yets
  (woman) afstraleeka
automatic afta-mateechyeskee
away: is it far away? eta dalyeko?
  go away! ookhadeet-ye!
awful oozhasni
axe tapor

baby ryebyonak
back: at the back szadee
  (body) speena
bad plakhoy
bakery boolachna-ya
balalaika balalika
balcony balkon
ball myach

105

ballet balyet
ball-point pen shareekava-ya roochka
Baltic (*states*) preebalteeka
banana banan
band (*musicians*) arkyestr
bandage beent
bank bank
banknote banknota
bar bar
　bar of chocolate pleetka shakalada
barber's pareekmakhyerska-ya
basement padval
basin (*sink*) rakaveena
basket karzeena
bath vana
　to have a bath preeneemat' vanoo
bathing hat koopal'na-ya shapachka
bathroom vana-ya
battery bataryayka
beach plyash
beans fasol'
beard barada
because patamoo shto
bed kravat'
bed linen pastyel'na-ye byel'yo
bedroom spal'nya
beef gavyadeena
beer peeva
before do
beginner nacheena-yooshee
behind za
beige byezhevi
bell (*church*) kolakal
　(*door*) zvanok
below pod
belt po-yas
beside okala
best loochee

better looch-ye
between myezhdoo
bicycle vyelaseepyed
big bal'shoy
bikini koopal'neek
bill shyot
bird pteetsa
birthday dyen' razhdyenee-ya
　happy birthday! zdnyom razhdyenee-ya!
biscuit pyechyen'ye
bite (*verb*) koosat'
　(*noun*) ookoos
　(*by insect*) ookoos nasyekomava
bitter gor'kee
black chyorni
blackcurrant chyorna-ya smarodeena
Black Sea chyorna-ye mor-ye
blanket adye-yala
bleach (*verb: hair*) visvyetleet'
blind (*cannot see*) slyepoy
blister valdir
blood krof'
blouse blooska
blue seenee
boat parakhot
　(*smaller*) lotka
body tyela
bone kost'
bonnet (*car*) kapot
book (*noun*) kneega
　(*verb*) zakazivat'
booking office kasa
bookshop kneezhni magazeen
boot (*car*) bagazhneek
　(*footwear*) sapok
border graneetsa
boring skooshni
born; I was born in... (*male*) ya radeelsa v...
　(*female*) ya radeelas' v...

both oba
  both of them anee oba
  both of us mi oba
  both... and... ee... ee...
bottle bootilka
bottle-opener shtopar
bottom dno
bowl chashka
box karopka
boy mal'cheek
boyfriend drook
bra byoostgal'tyer
bracelet braslyet
brandy kan'yak
bread khlyep
break (*noun*) pyeryerif
  (*verb*) lamat'
breakdown (*car*) palomka
  (*nervous*) nyervna-ye rastroystva
breakfast zaftrak
breathe dishat'
  I can't breathe mnye troodna
  dishat'
bridge most
briefcase partfyel'
British breetanskee
brochure brashyoora
broken slomani
  broken leg slomana-ya naga
brooch brosh
brother brat
brown kareechnyevi
bruise seenyak
brush (*noun*) shyotka
  (*paint*) keest'
bucket vyedro
bug (*in room*) klop
building zdaneeye
Bulgarian balgarskee
burglar vor
burn (*verb*) abzheegat'
  (*noun*) azhok

bus aftoboos
bus station aftoboosna-ya
  stantsee-ya
business dyela
  it's none of your business eta
  nye vashe dyela
busy (*occupied*) zanyat
but no
butcher myasnoy magazeen
butter masla
button poogaveetsa
buy pakoopat'
by: by the window okala akna
Byelorussia byelaroosee-ya

cabbage kapoosta
café kafe
cake kyeks
calculator kal'koolyatar
call (*summon*) zvat'
  (*telephone*) zvaneet'
  what's it called? kak eta
  naziva-yetsa?
camera fata-aparat
campsite kyempeeng
can (*tin*) banka
  can I have...? mozhna...?
Canada kanada
Canadian kanatskee
  (*man*) kanadyets
  (*female*) kanatka
cancer rak
candle svyecha
canoe kanoe
cap (*bottle*) propka
  (*hat*) kyepka
car masheena
caravan dom-aftafoorgon
card atkritka
cardigan kofta
careful astarozhni

be careful! astarozhna!
carpet kavyor
carriage (*train*) vagon
carrot markof'
case chyemadan
cash naleechniye
  (*coins*) manyeti
  to pay cash plateet'
  naleechnimee
Caspian Sea kaspeeska-ye mor-ye
cassette kasyeta
cassette player magneetafon
castle zamak
cat koshka
cathedral sabor
Caucasus kafkas
cauliflower tsvyetna-ya kapoosta
cave pyeshyera
cemetery kladbeeshe
centre tsyentr
certificate oodastavyeryeneeye
chair stool
chambermaid gorneechna-ya
change (*noun: money*) abmyen
  (*verb: clothes*) pyerye-adyevat'sa
  (*verb: money*) razmyenyat'
cheap dyeshyovi
cheers! (*toast*) vashe zdarov'ye!
cheese sir
chemist (*shop*) aptyeka
cheque chyek
cheque book chyekava-ya
  kneeshka
cherry veeshnya
chess shakhmati
chest groot'
chewing gum zhevatyel'na-ya
  ryezeenka
chicken kooreetsa
child ryebyonak
children dyetee
China keetI

chips kartofyel' free
chocolate shakalat
  box of chocolates karopka
  shakaladnikh kanfyet
chop (*food*) atbeevna-ya
  (*cut*) roobeet'
Christian name eemya
church tserkaf'
cigar seegara
cigarette seegaryeta
cinema keeno
circus tseerk
city gorat
city centre tsyentr gorada
class klas
classical music
  klaseechyeska-ya moozika
clean cheesti
clear (*obvious*) yasni
  is that clear? eta yasna?
clever oomni
clock chasi
close (*near*) bleeskee
  (*stuffy*) dooshni
  (*verb*) zakrivat'
  the shop is closed magazeen
  zakrit
clothes adyezhda
club kloop
coach aftoboos
  (*of train*) vagon
coach station aftoboosna-ya
  stantsee-ya
coat pal'to
coathanger vyeshalka
cockroach tarakan
coffee kof-ye
coin manyeta
cold (*illness*) greep
  (*adj*) khalodni
collar varatneek
collection (*stamps etc*) kalyektsee-ya

colour tsvyet
colour film tsvyetna-ya plyonka
comb (*noun*) raschyoska
   (*verb*) preechyosivat'sa
come preekhadeet'
   I come from... ya eez...
   come here! ecdeet-ye syooda!
communication cord stop-kran
Communist Party
   kamooneesteechyeska-ya
   partee-ya
compartment koope
complicated slozhni
concert kantsyert
conductor (*bus*) kandooktar
   (*orchestra*) deereezhyor
congratulations! pazdravlya-yoo!
connection (*rail*) pyeryesatka
constipation zapor
consulate konsoolstva
contact lenses kantaktniye leenzi
contraceptive prateeva-
   zachatachna-ye sryedstva
cook (*noun*) povar
   (*verb*) gatoveet'
cooking utensils kookhaniye
   preenadlyezhnastee
cool prakhladni
cork propka
corkscrew shtopar
corner oogal
corridor kareedor
cosmetics kasmyeteeka
Cossack kazak
cost (*verb*) sto-eet'
   what does it cost? skol'ka eta
   sto-eet?
cotton khlopak
cotton wool vata
cough (*verb*) kashlyat'
   (*noun*) kashel'
country (*state*) strana

   (*not town*) dyeryevnya
course: of course kanyeshna
cousin (*male*) dva-yooradni brat
   (*female*) dva-yooradna-ya syestra
crab krap
cream sleefkee
credit card kryedeetna-ya
   kartachka
crew ekeepash
Crimea krim
crisps cheepsi
crowded pyeryepolnyeni
cruise kroo-ees
crutches kastilee
cry (*weep*) plakat'
   (*shout*) kreechat'
cucumber agooryets
cufflinks zapankee
cup chashka
cupboard shkaf
curtain zanavyeska
Customs tamozhnya
cut (*noun*) paryez
   (*verb*) ryezat'

dad papa
damp siroy
dance tanyets
dangerous apasni
dark tyomni
date cheeslo
daughter doch'
day dyen'
dead myortvi
deaf glookhoy
dear daragoy
deckchair shezlong
deep gloobokee
delay zadyershka
deliberately narochna
dentist zoobnoy vrach
dentures pratyez

deodorant dyezadarant
depart (*verb*) oo-yezhat'
department store ooneevyermak
develop (*a film*) pra-yavlyat'
diamond breelee-ant
diarrhoea panos
diary dnyevneek
dictionary slavar'
die oomeerat'
diesel deezyel
diet dee-yeta
different (*other*) droogoy
  (*various*) razni
  that's different eta
  droogo-ye dyela
difficult troodni
dining room stalova-ya
dinner (*evening meal*) oozheen
directory (*telephone*) tyelyefoni
  spravachneek
dirty gryazni
disabled eenvaleet
dive niryat'
diving board trampleen
divorced (*male*) razvyedyoni
  (*female*) razvyedyena-ya
do dyelat'
doctor vrach
document dakoomyent
dog sabaka
doll kookla
dollar dolar'
door dvyer'
double room nomyer
  zdvoospal'nay kravat'yoo
down fnees
dress plat'ye
drink (*verb*) peet'
  (*noun*) napeetak
drinking water peet'yeva-ya vada
drive (*verb*) vadeet'
driver vadeetyel'

driving licence vadeetyel'skeeye
  prava
drunk p'yani
dry sookhoy
dry cleaner kheemcheestka
dummy (*for baby*) soska
during va-vryemya
dustbin moosarni yasheek
duster tryapka dlya pilee
duty-free byesposhleena-ya
  targovlya

each (*every*) kazhdi
  twenty roubles each dvatsat'
  rooblyay kazhdi
ear ookha
  (*plural*) ooshee
early rana
earrings syer'gee
east vastok
Easter paskha
easy lyokhkee
eat yest'
egg yitso
elastic ryezeenka
elbow lokat'
electric elyektreechyeskee
electricity elyektreechyestva
else: something else shto-ta yeshyo
  someone else kto-ta yeshyo
  somewhere else gdye-ta yeshyo
elevator leeft
embarrassed smooshyoni
embassy pasol'stva
emerald eezoomroot
emergency exit zapasnoy vikhat
empty poostoy
end kanyets
engaged (*couple*) pamolvlyeni
  (*occupied*) zanyat
engine (*motor*) dveegatyel'
England anglee-ya

English angleeskee
   (*language*) angleeskee yazik
Englishman angleechaneen
Englishwoman angleechanka
enlargement oovyeleechyeneeye
enough dastatachna
enter fkhadeet'
entertainment razvlyechyeneeye
entrance fkhot
envelope kanvyert
especially asobyena
Europe yevropa
evening vyechyer
every kazhdi
everyone fsye
everything fsyo
everywhere vyezd-ye
example preemyer
  for example napreemyer
excellent atleechni
excess baggage pyeryevyes
  bagazha
exchange (*verb*) myenyat'
exchange rate valyootni koors
excursion ekskoorsee-ya
excuse me! (*to get past*)
  razryesheet-ye!
  (*to get attention*) prasteet-ye!
exhibition vistafka
exit vikhat
expensive daragoy
explain abyasnyat'
eye drops glazniye kaplee
eyes glaza

fabric tkan'
face leetso
fact fakt
faint (*unclear*) tooskli
  (*verb*) tyeryat' saznaneeye
fair (*funfair*) yarmarka
  (*just*) spravyedleevi

fall (*verb*) padat'
false teeth pratyez
family syem'ya
fan (*ventilator*) vyenteelyatar
  (*enthusiast*) balyel'sheek
far dalyeko
fare sto-eemast' pra-yezda
farm fyerma
farmer fyermyer
fashion moda
fast bistro
fat (*person*) tolsti
  (*on meat etc*) zheer
father atyets
feel (*touch*) trogat'
  I feel hot mnye zharka
  I don't feel well mnye plokha
feet nogee
felt-tip pen flamastyer
female zhenskee
ferry parom
fever leekharatka
few nyeskal'ka
fiancé zheneekh
fiancée nyevyesta
field pol-ye
fill in zapalnyat'
filling (*tooth*) plomba
fill up napolnyat'
film (*cinema*) feel'm
  (*camera*) plyonka
filter feeltr
find (*verb*) nakhadeet'
finger palyets
Finland feenlyandee-ya
fire (*blaze*) pazhar
fire exit pazharni vikhat
fire extinguisher agnyetoosheetyel'
firework salyoot
first pyervi
first aid skora-ya pomash'
first floor ftaroy etash

111

fish riba
fishing ribna-ya lovlya
  to go fishing khadeet' na ribalkoo
fishing rod oodachka
fishmonger ribni magazeen
fizzy sheepoochee
flag flak
flash (*camera*) fspishka
flat (*level*) ploskee
  (*apartment*) kvarteera
flavour fkoos
flea blakha
flight ryays
floor (*of building*) etash
  (*of room*) pol
flour mooka
flower tsvyetok
flu greep
flute flyayta
fly (*verb*) lyetyet'
  (*insect*) mookha
fog tooman
folk music narodna-ya moozika
food yeda
food poisoning peeshevo-ye atravlyeneeye
foot naga
  on foot pyeshkom
football footbol
  (*ball*) footbol'ni myach
for dlya
  for me dlya myenya
  what for? dlya chyevo?
forbid zapryeshat'
foreigner (*man*) eenastranyets
  (*woman*) eenastranka
forest lyes
fork veelka
fortnight dvye nyedyelee
fountain pen aftaroochka
fourth chyetvyorti

fracture pyeryelom
free svabodni
  (*no cost*) byesplatni
freezer marazeel'neek
French frantsooskee
fridge khaladeel'neek
friend (*male*) drook
  (*female*) padrooga
friendly droozheskee
from ot
  I'm from London ya eez londana
front: in front of pyeryet
frost maros
frozen (*person*) zamyorshee
fruit frookt
fruit juice frooktovi sok
fry zhareet'
frying pan skavarada
full polni
  I'm full (*male*) ya sit
  (*female*) ya sita
funny (*amusing*) smyeshnoy
  (*odd*) strani
fur myekh
fur hat myekhava-ya shapka
furniture myebel'

game eegra
garage (*service station*) stantsee-ya tyekh-absloozheevanee-ya
  (*petrol station*) byenzakalonka
  (*parking*) garazh
garden sat
garlic chyesnok
gay (*homosexual*) galooboy
gear pyeryedacha
gents (*toilet*) mooshskoy too-alyet
Georgia groozee-ya
German nyemyetskee
get (*fetch*) dastavat'
  have you got...? oo vas yest'...?
  to get the train oospyet' na po-yest

get back (*return*) vazvrashat'sa
get in/on (*to transport*) sadeet'sa
get out vikhadeet'
get up (*rise*) fstavat'
gift padarak
gin dzheen
girl dyevooshka
girlfriend padrooga
give davat'
glad rat
  I'm glad (*male*) ya rat
  (*female*) ya rada
glass (*for drinking*) stakan
  (*material*) styeklo
glasses achkee
gloves pyerchatkee
glue klay
goggles zasheetniye achkee
gold zolata
good kharoshee
  good! kharasho
goodbye dasveedanee-ya
government praveetyel'stva
granddaughter fnoochka
grandfather dyedooshka
grandmother babooshka
grandson fnook
grapes veenagrat
grass trava
Great Britain
  vyeleekabreetanee-ya
green zyelyoni
grey syeri'
grill greel'
grocer (*shop*) bakalye-ya
ground floor pyervi etash
group groopa
guarantee (*noun*) garantee-ya
  (*verb*) garanteeravat'
guard storash
guest gost'
guide book pootyevadeetyel'

guitar geetara
gun (*rifle*) roozh'yo

hair volasi
haircut streeshka
hairdresser pareekmakhyer
hair dryer fyen
hair spray lak dlya valos
half palaveena
  half an hour palchasa
ham vyetcheena
hammer malatok
hand rooka
handbag damska-ya soomka
handkerchief nasavoy platok
handle (*door*) roochka
handsome kraseevi
hangover pakhmyel'ye
happy shasleevi
harbour gavan'
hard tvyordi
  (*difficult*) troodni
hat shlyapa
have eemyet'
  I don't have... oo myenya nyet...
  have you got...? oo vas yest'...?
  I have to go now mnye para
hayfever syena-ya leekharatka
he on
head galava
headache galavna-ya bol'
health zdarov'ye
hear slishat'
hearing aid slookhavoy apparat
heart syertse
heart attack syerdyechni preestoop
heating ataplyeneeye
heavy tyazholi
heel (*foot*) pyatka
  (*shoe*) kablook
hello zdrastvooyt-ye
help (*noun*) pomash'

113

(*verb*) pamagat'
help! pamageet-ye!
her: it's her eta ana
  for her dlya nye-yo
  give it to her atdit-ye yay
  her bag/bags ye-yo soomka/
  soomkee
  her house ye-yo dom
  her shoes ye-yo tooflee
  it's hers eta ye-yo
high visokee
hill kholm
him: it's him eta on
  for him dlya nyevo
  give it to him atdit-ye yemoo
hire prakat
his: his book/books yevo
  kneega/kneegee
  his house yevo dom
  it's his eta yevo
history eestoree-ya
hitch-hike pootyeshestvavat'
  afta-stopam
hobby khobee
holiday otpoosk
home dom
  at home doma
honest chyesni
honey myot
honeymoon myedovi myesyats
hope (*verb*) nadyeyat'sa
  (*noun*) nadyezhda
horn (*car*) seegnal
  (*animal*) rok
horrible oozhasni
horse loshat'
hospital bal'neetsa
hot water bottle gryelka
hour chas
house dom
how? kak?
  how much? skol'ka?

Hungary vyengree-ya
hungry: I'm hungry (*male*) ya
  galodyen
  (*female*) ya galodna
hurry: I'm in a hurry ya spyeshoo
hurt (*verb*) balyet'
husband moosh

I ya
ice lyot
ice cream marozhena-ye
ice hockey khakay
ice lolly frooktova-ye marozhena-ye
ice skates kan'kee
ice skating katat'sa na kan'kakh
icicle sasool'ka
icon eekona
if yeslee
ill (*male*) bolyen
  (*female*) bal'na
illness balyezn'
immediately nyemyedlyena
important vazhni
impossible nyevazmozhna
in v
  in English pa-angleeskee
  in the hotel v gasteeneets-ye
Indian eendeeskee
indicator ookazatyel' pavarota
indigestion nyesvaryeneeye
  zhelootka
infection eenfyektsee-ya
information eenfarmatsee-ya
information office spravachna-ye
  byooro
injection eenyektsee-ya
injury rana
ink chyerneela
insect nasyekoma-ye
insect repellent sryedstva ot
  nasyekomikh
insomnia byesoneetsa

insurance strakhofka
interesting eentyeryesni
international myezhdoo-narodni
interpret pyeryevadeet'
interpreter pyeryevotcheek
into v
invitation preeglasheneeye
Ireland eerlandee-ya
Irish eerlantskee
Irishman eerlandyets
Irishwoman eerlantka
iron (metal) zhelyeza
   (for clothes) ootyook
island ostraf
it eta
itch (noun) chyesotka
   it itches chyeshetsa

jacket peedzhak
jam varyenye
jazz dzhas
jealous ryevneevi
jeans dzheensi
jellyfish myedooza
jeweller's yoovyeleerni
   magazeen
job rabota
jog (verb) byegat' troostsoy
joke shootka
journey pa-yestka
jump (verb) prigat'
jumper dzhempyer
just tol'ka

key klyooch
kidney pochka
kilo keelo
kilometre keelamyetr
kind dobri
kitchen kookhnya
knee kalyena
knife nosh

knit vyazat'
know: I don't know ya nye
   zna-yoo
Kremlin kryeml'

label eteekyetka
lace kroozheva
laces (of shoe) shnoorkee
ladies (toilet) zhenskee too-alyet
lake ozyera
lamb (meat) baraneena
lamp lampa
lampshade abazhoor
land (noun) zyemlya
   (verb) preezyemlyat'sa
language yazik
large bal'shoy
last (final) paslyednee
   last week na proshlay nyedyel-ye
   last month fproshlam myesyats-ye
   at last! nakanyets!
late: it's getting late pozna
   the bus is late aftoboos
   apazdiva-yet
later pozhe
laugh smyeyat'sa
launderette prachyechna-ya
   sama-absloozheevaneeye
laundry (place) prachyechna-ya
   (dirty clothes) gryazna-ye byel'yo
lavatory too-alyet
laxative slabeetyel'na-ye
lazy lyeneevi
leaf leest
leaflet leestofka
learn (language) eezoochat'
leather kozha
leave (something somewhere)
   astavlyat'
   (by transport) oo-yezhat'
   (on foot) ookhadeet'
left (not right) lyevi

there's nothing left neechyevo nye astalas'
left luggage (*locker*) kamyera khranyenee-ya
leg naga
lemon leemon
lemonade leemanat
length dleena
Lenin's Mausoleum mavzalyay lyeneena
lens leenza
less myen'she
lesson oorok
letter pees'mo
letterbox pachtovi yasheek
lettuce salat-latook
library beeblee-atyeka
licence vadeetyel'skeeye prava
life zheezn'
lift (*in building*) leeft
light svyet
  (*not heavy*) lyokhkee
  (*not dark*) svyetli
light bulb lampachka
lighter zazheegalka
lighter fuel byenzeen dlya zazheegalkee
like: I like you ti mnye nraveesh'sa
  I like swimming mnye nraveetsa plavat'
  it's like... eta kak...
lip gooba
lipstick goobna-ya pamada
liqueur leekyor
list speesak
listen slooshat'
Lithuania leetva
litre leetr
litter moosar
little (*small*) malyen'kee
  a little nyemnoga

liver pyechyen'
lollipop lyedyenyets
long dleeni
look at smatryet'
look for eeskat'
lorry groozaveek
lose tyeryat'
lost property byooro nakhodak
lot: a lot mnoga
loud gromkee
lounge gasteena-ya
love (*noun*) lyoobof'
  (*verb*) lyoobeet'
low neezkee
luck oodacha
  good luck! zhela-yoo oodachee!
luggage bagazh
luggage rack bagazhna-ya polka
lunch abyet

magazine zhoornal
mail pochta
make dyelat'
make-up greem
male mooshskoy
man mooshcheena
manager admeeneestratar
many mnoga
map karta
  a map of Moscow karta maskvi
marble mramar
margarine margareen
market rinak
married (*male*) zhenat
  (*female*) zamoozhem
mascara toosh' dlya ryesneets
mass (*church*) myesa
match (*light*) speechka
  (*sport*) match
material (*cloth*) tkan'
matter: it doesn't matter nyevazhna
mattress matras

maybe mozhet bit'
me: it's me eta ya
  for me dlya myenya
  give it to me dit-ye mnye
meal yeda
meat myasa
mechanic myekhaneek
medicine lyekarstva
meet fstryechat'
meeting fstryecha
melon dinya
menu myenyoo
message sa-abshyeneeye
midday poldyen'
middle: in the middle
  pasyeryedeen-ye
midnight polnach'
milk malako
mine: it's mine eta ma-yo
mineral water meenyeral'na-ya
  vada
minute meenoota
mirror zyerkala
Miss mees
miss (verb: train etc) apazdivat'
mistake asheepka
  to make a mistake asheebat'sa
monastery manastir'
money dyen'gee
month myesyats
monument pamyatneek
moon loona
more bol'she
morning ootra
  in the morning ootram
mosaic mazayka
Moscow maskva
mosquito kamar
mother mat'
motorbike matatseekl
motorway afta-strada
mountain gara

moustache oosi
mouth rot
move dveegat'sa
  don't move! nye dveegityes'!
  (house) pyerye-yezhat'
movie feel'm
Mr gaspadeen
Mrs gaspazha
much mnoga
  not much nyemnoga
  much better/slower garazda
  looch-ye/myedlyenye-ye
mug krooshka
mum mama
museum moozyay
mushroom greep
music moozika
musical instrument moozikal'ni
  eenstroomyent
musician moozikant
mussels meedee
must (male) dolzhen
  (female) dalzhna
mustard garcheetsa
my: my house moy dom
  my bag ma-ya soomka
  my keys ma-ee klyoochee

nail (metal) gvozd'
  (finger) nogat'
nail file peelka dlya nagtyay
nail polish lak dlya nagtyay
name (Christian) eemya
  (surname) fameelee-ya
nappy pyelyonka
narrow oozkee
near: near the door okala dvyeree
  near London okala londana
necessary noozhni
neck she-ya
necklace azheryel'ye
need (verb) noozhdat'sa

I need... mnye noozhna...
  there's no need eta nyenoozhna
needle eegla
negative (*photo*) nyegateef
nephew plyemyaneek
never neekagda
new novi
news novastee
newsagent gazyetni kee-osk
newspaper gazyeta
New Zealand nova-ya
  zyelandee-ya
New Zealander (*man*)
  navazyelandyets
  (*woman*) navazyelantka
next slyedoo-yooshee
  next week na slyedoo-yooshay
  nyedyel-ye
  next month fslyedoo-yooshem
  myesyatse
  what next? shto dal'she?
nice preeyatni
niece plyemyaneetsa
night noch'
nightclub nachnoy kloop
nightdress nachna-ya
  roobashka
night porter nachnoy dyezhoorni
no (*response*) nyet
  I have no money oo myenya
  nyet dyenyek
noisy shoomni
normal abichni
north syevyer
Northern Ireland syevyerna-ya
  eerlandee-ya
nose nos
not nye
notebook zapeesna-ya kneega
nothing neechyevo
notice abyavlyeneeye
novel raman

now tyepyer'
nowhere neegd-ye
number nomyer
nurse myedsyestra
nut (*fruit*) aryekh

occasionally eenagda
occupation prafyesee-ya
occupied zanyat
ocean akye-an
office kantora
often chasta
oil masla
ointment maz'
OK ladna
old stari
  how old are you? skol'ka vam
  lyet?
olive masleena
omelette amlyet
on na
one adeen
onion look
only tol'ka
open (*verb*) atkrivat'
  (*adj*) atkriti
opera opyera
opposite: opposite the hotel
  naproteef gasteeneetsi
optician opteeka
or eelee
orange (*colour*) aranzhevi
  (*fruit*) apyel'seen
orange juice apyel'seenavi sok
orchestra arkyestr
order (*in restaurant*) zakazivat'
  out of order nye fparyatk-ye
ordinary (*normal*) abichni
other droogoy
our nash
  it's ours eta nashe
out: he's out yevo nyet

outside na __oo__leets-ye
over (*above*) nad
   (*more than*) __bol__'she chyem
   over there tam
overtake abgan__yat__'

pack of cards ka__lo__da kart
package pak__yet__
   (*parcel*) pa__si__lka
packet __pa__chka
page stra__nee__tsa
pain bol'
paint (*noun*) __kra__ska
painting kar__tee__na
pair __pa__ra
Pakistani pakees__ta__nskee
palace dva__ryets__
pale bl__yed__ni
pancakes blee__ni__
paper boo__ma__ga
parcel pa__si__lka
pardon? pras__teet__-ye?
parents rad__ee__tyelee
park (*noun*) park
   (*verb*) sta__veet__' ma__shee__noo
part chast'
party (*celebration*) vyechyere__e__nka
   (*political*) par__tee__-ya
passenger pasa__zheer__
passport __pa__sport
path tra__pee__nka
patronymic __otchyes__tva
pavement tra__too__-ar
pay pla__teet__'
peace meer
peach pyer__seek__
peanuts ara__khees__
pear gr__oo__sha
pearl zhem__chook__
peas ga__rokh__
pedestrian pyeshekh__ot__
pen r__oo__chka

pencil karan__dash__
penknife pyer__acheeni nosh__
pensioner pyensee-an__yer__
people ly__oo__dee
pepper py__eryets__
per: per night za__nach__'
perfect pryevas__khodni__
perfume dook__hee__
perhaps __mozhet__ bit'
perm za__veefka__ pyerman__yent__
permission razryesh__eneeye__
petrol byen__zeen__
petrol station byenzaka__lonka__
photograph (*noun*) fatagra__fee__-ya
   (*verb*) fatagraf__eeravat__'
photographer fat__ograf__
phrase book razga__vorneek__
piano fartyep'__yana__
picnic peek__neek__
piece k__oo__sok
pillow pad__oo__shka
pilot pee__lot__
pin bool__afka__
pine (*tree*) __sasna__
pineapple ana__nas__
ping-pong peeng-p__ong__
pink __rozavi__
pipe (*for smoking*) tr__oopka__
   (*for water*) troobapr__ovat__
pizza __peetsa__
place my__esta__
plain pras__toy__
plant rastyen__eeye__
plaster (*for cut*) plas__tir__'
plastic plas__teekavi__
plastic bag plas__teekavi__ pak__yet__
plate tar__yelka__
platform plat__forma__
play (*noun: theatre*) p'__yesa__
   (*verb*) eegr__at__'
please pa__zhalsta__
plug (*electrical*) sht__yepsyel__'

119

(*sink*) propka
plum sleeva
pocket karman
poison atravlyeneeye
Poland pol'sha
police meeleetsee-ya
police station atdyelyeneeye
   meeleetsee-ya
policeman meeleetsee-anyer
politics paleeteeka
pollution zagryaznyeneeye
poor byedni
   (*bad quality*) plakhoy
pop music pop moozika
popular papoolyarni
pork sveeneena
port (*harbour*) port
porter (*for luggage*) naseel'sheek
possible vazmozhni
post (*noun*) pochta
   (*verb*) pasilat'
post box pachtovi yasheek
postcard atkritka
poster plakat
post office pochta
postman pachtal'on
potato kartofyel'
poultry pteetsa
pound foont
powder (*washing*) parashok
   (*talcum*) poodra
pram dyetska-ya kalyaska
prawn kryevyetka
pregnant byeryemyena-ya
prescription ryetsept
present padarak
pretty kraseevi
price tsyena
priest svyashyeneek
private chasni
problem prablyema
profession prafyesee-ya

public abshyestvyeni
pull tyanoot'
puncture prakol
pure cheesti
purple fee-alyetavi
purse kashelyok
push talkat'
put klast'
pyjamas peezhama

quality kachyestva
quantity kaleechyestva
quay preechal
question vapros
queue (*noun*) ochyeryet'
   (*verb*) stayat' vochyeryedee
quick bistri
quiet teekhee
quite (*fairly*) davol'na
   (*fully*) safsyem

radiator batarye-ya
radio radee-o
radish ryedeeska
railway line zhelyezna-darozhna-ya
   leenee-ya
rain dosht'
raincoat plash'
raisins eezyoom
rare (*uncommon*) ryetkee
   (*steak*) skrov'yoo
rat krisa
razor breetva
razor blades breetvyeniye
   lyezvee-ya
read cheetat'
ready gatof
real nasta-yashee
rear lights zadneeye fari
receipt chyek
receive paloochat'
receptionist dyezhoorni

recommend ryekamyendavat'
record (*music*) plasteenka
  (*sporting etc*) ryekort
record player pra-eegrivatyel'
red krasni
Red Square krasna-ya ploshat'
relative rodstvyeneek
relax atdikhat'
religion ryeleegee-ya
remember pomneet'
  I don't remember ya nye
  pomnyoo
rent (*verb*) naneemat'
reservation zakas
reserve zakazivat'
rest (*remainder*) astatak
  (*relax*) otdikh
restaurant ryestaran
return (*come back*) vazvrashat'sa
  (*give back*) vazvrashat'
return ticket abratni beelyet
rice rees
rich bagati
right (*correct*) praveel'ni
  (*direction*) pravi
  on the right naprava
ring (*telephone*) zvaneet'
  (*wedding etc*) kal'tso
ripe zryeli
river ryeka
road daroga
rock (*stone*) skala
  (*music*) rok
roll (*bread*) boolachka
Romania roominee-ya
roof krisha
room komnata
  (*in hotel*) nomyer
  (*space*) myesta
rope vyeryofka
rose roza
round (*circular*) kroogli

  it's my round moy chyeryot
rowing boat vyosyel'na-ya lotka
rubber (*eraser*) ryezeenka
  (*material*) ryezeena
rubbish moosar
ruby (*stone*) roobeen
rucksack ryookzak
rug (*mat*) kovreek
  (*blanket*) adye-yala
ruins roo-eeni
ruler (*for drawing*) leenyayka
rum rom
run (*person*) byezhat'
Russia rasee-ya
Russian (*adjective*) rooskee
  (*language*) rooskee yazik
  (*man*) rooskee
  (*woman*) rooska-ya
Russian Orthodox Church
  rooska-ya pravaslavna-ya tserkaf'

sad groosni
safe byezapasni
safety pin angleeska-ya boolafka
salad salat
salami kapchyona-ya kalbasa
sale (*at reduced prices*)
  raspradazha
salesperson pradavyets
salmon lasos'
salt sol'
same: the same dress to zhe
  plat'ye
  the same people tye zhe lyoodee
samovar samavar
sand pyesok
sandals sandalee
sandwich bootyerbrot
sanitary towels
  geegee-yeneechyeskeeye salfyetkee
sauce so-oos
saucepan kastryoolya

saucer blyoots-ye
sauna sa-oona
sausage saseeska
say gavareet'
  what did you say? shto vi skazalee?
  how do you say...? kak boodyet...?
scarf sharf
  (*head*) platok
scent dookhee
school shkola
scissors nozhneetsi
score shyot
Scotland shatlandee-ya
Scotsman shatlandyets
Scotswoman shatlantka
Scottish shatlantskee
screw veent
screwdriver atvyortka
sculpture skool'ptoora
sea mor-ye
seafood marskeeye pradookti
seat myesta
second (*of time*) syekoonda
  (*in series*) ftaroy
see veedyet'
  I can't see ya nye veezhoo
  I see! ya paneema-yoo!
seem kazat'sa
sell pradavat'
sellotape ® klyayka-ya lyenta
send pasilat'
separate atdyel'ni
serious syer'yozni
serve absloozheevat'
service (*restaurant*) absloozheevaneeye
  (*church*) sloozhba
serviette salfyetka
several nyeskal'ka
sew sheet'

shade tyen'
shallow myelkee
shampoo shampoon'
shape forma
sharp ostri
shave (*noun*) breet'yo
  (*verb*) breet'sa
shaving foam kryem dlya breet'ya
shawl shal'
she ana
sheet prastinya
sherry khyeryes
ship parakhot
shirt roobashka
shoe laces shnoorkee
shoe polish kryem dlya oboovee
shoes tooflee
shop magazeen
shore byerek
short karotkee
shorts shorti
shoulder plyecho
show pakazivat'
shower (*bath*) doosh
shrimp kryevyetka
shut (*verb*) zakrivat'
Siberia seebeer'
sick (*ill*) bal'noy
  I feel sick ya plokha syebya choostvoo-yoo
side (*edge*) starana
sidelights padfarneekee
sights: the sights of... dasta-preemyechatyel'nastee...
sign znak
silk shyolk
silver (*metal*) syeryebro
simple prastoy
sing pyet'
single (*one*) adeen
  (*unmarried: man*) khalastoy
  (*woman*) nyezamoozhnya-ya

single room adnamyesni nomyer
sister syestra
sit down sadeet'sa
size razmyer
skates kan'kee
ski (*verb*) katat'sa na lizhakh
skid (*verb*) zanaseet'
skirt yoopka
skis lizhee
ski sticks lizhniye palkee
sky nyeba
sleep (*noun*) son
   (*verb*) spat'
   to go to bed lazheet'sa spat'
sleeper spal'ni vagon
sleeping bag spal'ni myeshok
sleeping pill snatvorna-ye
slippers tapachkee
slow myedlyeni
small malyen'kee
smell (*noun*) zapakh
   (*verb*) pakhnoot'
smile (*noun*) oolipka
   (*verb*) oolibat'sa
smoke (*noun*) dim
   (*verb*) kooreet'
snack zakooska
snow snyek
   it's snowing eedyot snyek
snow plough snyega-
   ooborachna-ya masheena
snowstorm snyezhna-ya boorya
so: so good tak kharasho
soap milo
socks naskee
soda water gazeerovana-ya vada
somebody kto-ta
somehow kak-ta
something shto-ta
sometimes eenagda
somewhere gdye-ta
son sin

song pyesnya
sorry! eezveeneet-ye!
   I'm sorry eezveeneet-ye
soup soop
south yook
souvenir soovyeneer
spade (*shovel*) lapata
spanner gayechni klyooch
spark plug zapal'na-ya svyecha
speak gavareet'
   do you speak...? vi gavareet-ye
   pa-...?
   I don't speak... ya nye gavaryoo
   pa-...
spectacles achkee
spend (*money*) trateet'
   (*time*) pravadeet'
spider pa-ook
spinach shpeenat
spine speena
spoon loshka
sport sport
sprain rastyazheneeye
spring (*mechanical*) ryesora
spy shpee-on
square (*town*) ploshat'
stadium stadee-on
stage stsena
stairs lyesneetsa
stalls (*theatre*) partyer
stamp marka
stand (*verb*) stayat'
star zvyezda
   (*film*) keenazvyezda
start (*verb*) nacheenat'
   (*noun*) nachala
station (*mainline terminal*) vagzal
   (*underground*) stantsee-ya
statue statoo-ya
stay (*verb*) astanavleevat'sa
steak beefshtyeks
steal krast'

it's been stolen ookralee
Steppes styep'
sting (noun) ookoos
  (verb) koosat'
  it stings baleet
stockings choolkee
stomach zheloodak
stomach ache bol' vzhelootk-ye
stop (something) astanavleevat'
  (come to a halt)
  astanavleevat'sa
  (bus stop) astanofka
  stop! stoy!
storm boorya
St. Petersburg sankt pyetyerboorg
strawberry kloobneeka
stream (small river) roochyay
street ooleetsa
string (cord) vyeryofka
  (guitar etc) stroona
student (male) stoodyent
  (female) stoodyentka
stupid gloopi
suburbs preegarat
suddenly vdrook
sugar sakhar
suit (noun) kastyoom
  it suits you vam eedyot
suitcase chyemadan
sun sontse
sunbathe zagarat'
sunburn solnyechni azhok
sunglasses solnyechniye achkee
sunny: it's sunny solnyechna
suntan zagar
suntan lotion masla dlya zagara
supermarket ooneevyersam
supper oozheen
supplement dapalnyeneeye
sure oovyeryeni
  are you sure? vi oovyeryeni?
surname fameelee-ya

surprise (verb) oodeevlyat'
sweat (noun) pot
  (verb) patyet'
sweet (not sour) slatkee
  (candy) kanfyetka
swim plavat'
swimming costume koopal'ni
  kastyoom
swimming pool basyayn
swimming trunks plafkee
switch viklyoochatyel'
synagogue seenagoga

table stol
tablet tablyetka
take brat'
take off (noun) atpravlyeneeye
talcum powder tal'k
talk (noun) razgavor
  (verb) razgavareevat'
tall visokee
tampon tampon
tap kran
taste fkoos
tea chı
tea towel pasoodna-ye palatyentse
team kamanda
telegram tyelyegrama
telephone (noun) tyelyefon
  (verb) zvaneet'
telephone box tyelyefon-aftamat
television tyelyeveezar
temperature tyempyeratoora
tennis tyenees
tent palatka
than chyem
thank (verb) blagadareet'
  thanks, thank you spaseeba
that: that bus tot aftoboos
  that woman ta zhensheena
  what's that? shto eta?
  I think that... ya dooma-yoo shto...

theatre tye-atr

their: their room eekh komnata
  it's theirs eta eekh

them: it's them eta anee
  for them dlya neekh
  give it to them atdit-ye eem

then tagda

there tam
  there is/are... eemye-yetsa/
    eemye-yootsa...
  is/are there...? zdyes' est'...?
  is there a bank here? zdyes'
    yest' bank?

thermometer gradoosneek

thermos flask tyermas

these: these things etee vyeshee
  these are mine eta ma-ee

they anee

thick (wide) tolsti

thief vor

thin tonkee

thing vyesh'

think doomat'
  I think so ya dooma-yoo shto
    da
  I'll think about it ya padooma-
    yoo ab etam

third trye'tee

thirsty: I'm thirsty ya khachoo
  peet'

this: this bus etat aftoboos
  this woman eta zhensheena
  what's this? shto eta?
  this is Mr.... eta gaspadeen...

those: those things tye vyeshee
  those are his eta yevo

throat gorla

throat pastilles tablyetkee at
  kashlya

through chyeryes

thunderstorm graza

ticket beelyet

ticket office beelyetna-ya kasa

tie (noun) galstook
  (verb) zavyazivat'

tights kalgotkee

time vryemya
  what's the time? katori chas?

timetable raspeesaneeye

tin kansyervna-ya banka

tin opener kansyervni nosh

tip (money) cha-yeviye

tired oostali
  I'm tired (male) ya oostal
    (female) ya oostala

tissues boomazhniye salfyetkee

to: to England vanglee-yoo
  to the station na vagzal
  to the doctor k vrachoo

toast padzharyeni khlyep

tobacco tabak

today syevodnya

together fmyest-ye

toilet too-alyet

toilet paper too-alyetna-ya boomaga

tomato pameedor

tomato juice tamatni sok

tomorrow zaftra

tongue yazik

tonic toneek

tonight syevodnya vyechyeram

too (also) tagzhe
  (excessive) sleeshkam

tooth zoop

toothache zoobna-ya bol'

toothbrush zoobna-ya shyotka

toothpaste zoobna-ya pasta

torch fanareek

touch trogat'

tour ekskoorsee-ya

tourist tooreest

tourist office tooreesteechyeska-ye
  byooro

towel palatyentse

tower b<u>a</u>shnya
town g<u>o</u>rat
town hall rat<u>oo</u>sha
toy eegr<u>oo</u>shka
tracksuit tryeneer<u>o</u>vachni
  kast<u>yoo</u>m
tractor tr<u>a</u>ktar
tradition trad<u>ee</u>tsee-ya
traffic <u>oo</u>leechna-ye dveezh<u>e</u>neeye
traffic jam pr<u>o</u>pka
train p<u>o</u>-yest
tram tr<u>a</u>mvi
Trans-Siberian Express
  trans-seeb<u>e</u>erskee ekspr<u>e</u>s
translate pyeryevad<u>ee</u>t'
travel pootyesh<u>e</u>stvavat'
travel agency byoor<u>o</u>
  pootyesh<u>e</u>stvee
traveller's cheque dar<u>o</u>zhni chyek
tray padn<u>o</u>s
tree dyer<u>e</u>va
trolleybus tral<u>ya</u>yboos
trousers bry<u>oo</u>kee
truth pr<u>a</u>vda
try (*experimentally*) pr<u>o</u>bavat'
  (*endeavour*) star<u>a</u>t'sa
tunnel toon<u>ye</u>l'
Turkmenistan toorkmy<u>e</u>nee-ya
turn pavar<u>a</u>cheevat'
tweezers peents<u>e</u>t
typewriter peesh<u>oo</u>sha-ya
  mash<u>ee</u>nka
tyre sh<u>ee</u>na

Ukraine ookr<u>a</u>-eena
umbrella zont<u>ee</u>k
uncle dy<u>a</u>dya
uncomfortable nye-ood<u>o</u>bni
under pod
underground myetr<u>o</u>
underpants troos<u>i</u>
understand pan<u>ee</u>m<u>a</u>t'

I don't understand ya nye
  pan<u>ee</u>m<u>a</u>-yoo
underwear n<u>ee</u>zhn<u>ye</u>-ye byel'<u>yo</u>
United States sa-yedeeny<u>o</u>niye
  sht<u>a</u>ti
university oon<u>ee</u>vyerseet<u>ye</u>t
unmarried (*man*) nyezhen<u>a</u>t
  (*female*) nyez<u>a</u>moozhem
until do
unusual nye-ab<u>i</u>chni
upwards nav<u>ye</u>rkh
upstairs navyerkh<u>oo</u>
Urals oor<u>a</u>l
urgent sr<u>o</u>chni
us: it's us <u>e</u>ta mi
  it's for us <u>e</u>ta dlya nas
  give it to us d<u>i</u>t-ye nam
use (*noun*) oopatryebly<u>e</u>neeye
  (*verb*) oopatrye<u>bl</u>yat'
  it's no use nye rab<u>o</u>ta-yet
useful paly<u>e</u>zni
useless byespaly<u>e</u>zni
usual ab<u>i</u>chni
usually ab<u>i</u>chna

vacant (*room*) svab<u>o</u>dni
vacuum cleaner pily<u>e</u>sos
valid dyaystveet<u>ye</u>l'ni
valley dal<u>ee</u>na
valve kl<u>a</u>pan
vanilla van<u>ee</u>l'
vase v<u>a</u>za
veal tyel<u>ya</u>teena
vegetable <u>o</u>vash
vegetarian (*person*)
  vyegyetar<u>ee</u>-<u>a</u>nyets
very <u>o</u>chyen'
vest m<u>i</u>ka
view veet
villa v<u>ee</u>la
village dyer<u>ye</u>vnya
vinegar <u>oo</u>ksoos

violin skreepka
visa veeza
visit (*noun*) pasyesheneeye
  (*verb*) pasyeshat'
visitor pasyeteetyel'
  (*tourist*) tooreest
vitamin veetameen
vodka votka
voice golas
voltage napryazhenceye

wait zhdat'
waiter afeetsee-ant
  waiter! tavareesh afeetsee-ant!
waiting room zal azheedanee-ya
waitress afeetsee-antka
Wales oo-el's
walk (*noun: stroll*) pragoolka
  (*verb*) goolyat'
  to go for a walk eetee na
  pragoolkoo
wall styena
wallet boomazhneek
want khatyet'
  I want... ya khachoo...
war vina
wardrobe shkaf
warm tyopli
was: I was (*male*) ya bil
  (*female*) ya bila
  it was eta bila
washing powder steeral'ni
  parashok
washing-up liquid zheedkast'
  dlya mit'ya pasoodi
wasp asa
watch (*noun*) chasi
  (*verb*) smatryet'
water vada
waterfall vadapat
wave (*noun*) valna
  (*verb*) makhat'

we mi
weather pagoda
wedding svad'ba
week nyedyelya
welcome dabro pazhalavat'
  you're welcome pazhalsta
wellingtons ryezeenaviye sapagee
Welsh oo-el'skee
were: we were mi bilee
  you were vi bilee
  (*singular familiar: male*) ti bil
  (*female*) ti bila
  they were anee bilee
west zapat
  in the West na zapad-ye
wet mokri
what? shto?
wheel kalyeso
wheelchair eenvaleedna-ya kalyaska
when? kagda?
where? gdye?
which? kakoy?
while paka
whisky veeskee
white byeli
who? kto?
whole tseli
whose? chyay?
why? pachyemoo?
wide sheerokee
wife zhena
wild deekee
win vi-eegrivat'
wind vyetyer
window akno
wine veeno
wing krilo
wish zhelat'
with s
without byez
woman zhensheena
wonderful choodyesni

wood dyeryeva
wool sherst'
word slova
work (*noun*) rabota
  (*verb*) rabotat'
worry (*verb*) val'navat'sa
worse khoozhe
worst khoodshee
wrapping paper abyortachna-ya
  boomaga
wrist zapyast'ye
writing paper pachtova-ya
  boomaga
wrong nyepraveel'ni

year got
yellow zholti

yes da
yesterday fchyera
yet yeshyo
  not yet yeshyo nyet
you vi
  (*singular familiar*) ti
your vash
  (*singular familiar*) tvoy
  your room vash/tvoy nomyer
  your book vasha/tva-ya kneega
  your shoes vashee/tva-ee tooflee
yours: is this yours? eta vashe?/
  tva-yo?

zip molnee-ya
zoo za-apark